"How Shall They Hear?"

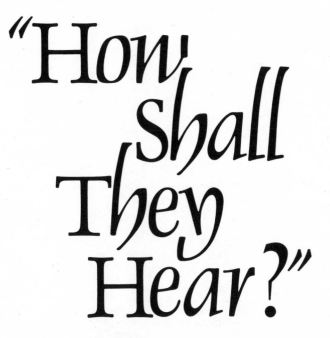

"How Shall They Hear?"

EFFECTIVE PREACHING FOR VITAL FAITH

Samuel D. Proctor

FOREWORD BY DAVID G. BUTTRICK

Judson Press ® Valley Forge

Library of Congress Cataloging-in-Publication Data
Proctor, Samuel D.
"How shall they hear?" : effective preaching for vital faith / by
Samuel D. Proctor.
    p.   cm.
1990 Lyman Beecher lectures on preaching. — Acknowledgments.
ISBN 0-8170-1172-2
    1. Preaching.   I. Title.   II. Title: Lyman Beecher lectures.
BV4222.P75   1992
251 — dc20   91-45275
                                                                CIP

Printed in the U.S.A.

07 06 05 04 03 02 01 00 99 98 97

12 11 10 9 8 7 6 5 4 3 2

Cover design by James Gerhard

Dedicated in grateful memory
to my sainted grandmother
Hattie Ann Virginia Proctor
and to my
great-grandfather
Rev. Zachariah Hughes,
a faithful pastor in
Norfolk, Virginia,
1879–1915

Contents

Acknowledgments 1
Foreword....................................... 3
1   Four Vital Faith Issues.................... 5
2   The Celebration of God's Presence and
    Participation in Human Affairs........ 19
3   The Assurance of Spiritual Renewal
    and Moral Wholeness 33
4   The Affirmation of Hope for a Genuine
    Human Community.................. 55
5   The Awareness of the Eternal in the
    Midst of Time...................... 81

Acknowledgments

My indebtedness as an interpreter of the Christian gospel for over fifty years is extensive, beginning with devoted, faithful parents, a sainted grandmother, and a great-grandfather whose labors for Christ were a legend during my childhood. It was Rev. Duel C. Rice, my pastor at the Bank Street Baptist Church in Norfolk, Virginia, who encouraged me to enter a career in ministry, and Rev. John B. Henderson, a later pastor of mine, who gave early and continuous support. My gratitude extends to others who were never told adequately what their influence meant to me: Dr. Harry Roberts, at Virginia State College during my turbulent sophomore year, and Dr. John M. Ellison of Virginia Union University, a mentor for over thirty years.

The faculties of Crozer Theological Seminary, Yale Divinity School, and The School of Theology of Boston University made theological study a high adventure and each preaching event a serious challenge.

The patience and forbearance of the congregations at the Pond Street Baptist Church in Providence, Rhode

1

Island (1945–1949), and the historic Abyssinian Baptist Church of New York City (1972–1989) were a loving constraint toward discipline and real accountability in the pulpit.

Several persons were kind enough to read these chapters and to lend helpful suggestions: Dr. Charles Booth, Dr. David Buttrick, Dr. Calvin Butts, Dr. Jean Dorgan, Dr. William Epps, Dean Forrest Harris, Dr. O. Clayton Johnson, Dr. Suzan Johnson, Mrs. Margaret Knispel, Dr. Mercile Lee, Dr. Mary Olson, Dr. Peter Paris, Dr. Benjamin Payton, Dr. Rosalyn Riggs, Dr. Terry Scherf, Dr. Wallace Smith, the Reverend Frederick Streets, Dr. Jewel Thompson, Dr. Daryl Ward, Dr. Renita Weems, and Dr. Jaqueline Young.

My wife, Bessie, and my four sons, Herbert, Timothy, Samuel, and Steven are a constant source of inspiration and constructive criticism; and my secretary, Mrs. Lorraine Smoller, has been unfailing in her service and loyalty.

The faculty of the Yale Divinity School and Dean Thomas W. Ogletree honored me far beyond my merit in inviting me to deliver the 1990 Lyman Beecher Lectures on Preaching. In doing so they placed me in a long procession of luminous preachers that began in May 1872. I remain humbly grateful for such an opportunity to refine my understanding of the preacher's task and to present the lectures in this modest publication.

I wish to thank Dr. David G. Buttrick, a colleague at Vanderbilt during my year as a visiting professor there, who was gracious enough to write a foreword.

> *Samuel D. Proctor*
> Anne Potter Wilson Visiting Professor
> The Divinity School
> Vanderbilt University
> Nashville, Tennessee

Foreword

A month ago Samuel Proctor spoke at a breakfast held in The Divinity School of Vanderbilt University. On the way out, a student looked back at Dr. Proctor with admiration and spoke: "He lifts you up," the student remarked. "He hands out hope."

Dr. Samuel Proctor has been lifting people up ever since 1945 when he began preaching in Pond Street Baptist Church, Providence, Rhode Island. Preacher, professor, author, twice university president, Sam Proctor has given significant leadership to the Peace Corps, the National Council of the Churches of Christ, the Office of Economic Opportunity, and the Institute for Services to Education. For years he held down two positions at the same time, either one of which would have daunted a lesser person: He was Martin Luther King, Jr., Professor at Rutgers University and, during the same fifteen years, pastor to the prestigious Abyssinian Baptist Church in New York City. But mostly Samuel Proctor has traveled the world giving us hope. "He lifts you up," the student said, and he does.

What is his secret? Sam Proctor is unusually alert; he is bright-eyed; he sees signs that other folks are apt to miss. Surely he has "eyes of faith" for, in an all-too-cynical world, he celebrates God's redemptive activity. He can point you toward where God is busy and open your eyes to see the same miracles of grace he himself has spotted—"he hands out hope."

Of course, he is deceptively smart. How do you speak the gospel to a wised-up, hoped-out twentieth-century world? How can a preacher talk of the kingdom, eternal life, or redemption in an age when the "otherness" of God has edged toward absence? Samuel Proctor has found a way and can show us lesser preachers how. He speaks; we can listen, indeed, listen and learn.

Well, I wish I could have been on hand for his 1990 Lyman Beecher Lectures. He preached them, of course, for they were meant to be preached. The real secret of Sam Proctor is that he is a true "gospeller," and as you hear him, the power of the gospel message positively radiates from him. He loves. He affirms. He affirms. He lifts. He hands out hope.

How do you listen to Samuel Proctor? Expectantly. Be ready to laugh like a lifted-up child for the fine, free Good News of the gospel message.

David G. Buttrick
The Divinity School
Vanderbilt University
Lent 1991

ONE

Four Vital Faith Issues

One of the oldest and most familiar exercises in which we regularly engage on Sunday mornings is the attentive, patient, serious, and reverent listening to sermons, those twenty- to forty-minute presentations of religious ideas and stimulants of moral and spiritual sentiments. From the lofty pulpits of elegant Gothic sanctuaries to the homemade lecterns in pulsating, tinted-window storefronts on cluttered ghetto avenues, preaching happens.

Whether the sermon is offered in a modern suburban church to six-figure-income parishioners or in a clapboard rural chapel to simple country folk, these exercises have certain elements in common. Often a sermon is a simple celebration, not new or startling, but a recitation of faithful sayings that send joy and spiritual satisfaction rippling through the pews. Some of the time it is purely to affirm and to edify—the call to a renewed commitment to the faith. At other times it may be to prophesy and to challenge—a prodding to action, an effort to break inertia, to confront apathy, or to rally to a just cause. Often it is somber and soothing, a balm in Gilead, a solace for troubled times, an assurance of the mystical presence of God. Much of it is simply instructional, an exegetical homily on a Bible verse or a dramatic retelling of the story of creation, of Samson, Ruth, Jonah, Job, the crucifixion of Jesus, or the conversion of Saul of Tarsus to the apostle Paul.

Preaching goes on.

Various polls tell us that we are mostly a believing people and that a large percentage attend churches and synagogues. This, however, says little about the content of what is heard or how well it is conveyed. While the general purposes of sermons are as listed above, no rigid criteria control the quality of the presentation.

The preparation of preachers varies greatly, as does the quality of the presentations. Some persons, in preparation for the preaching ministry, have been fortunate enough to have had an excellent college education as well as a complete seminary experience that included comprehensive training in biblical studies, the history of other religions, church history, and the psychology and philosophy of religion wherever and however it is practiced. Such an education may also have covered personal counseling, private and public ethics, and systematic theology—the coherent understanding of God's relationship with humankind.

Unfortunately, others come through a very narrow training program that shuts out insights from the natural sciences (the facts about God's creation!), that has contempt for findings of reliable and honest biblical research and scholarship, and that ignores the best in the disciplines of paleontology, archaeology, and anthropology. It is mainly anti-intellectual, makes no effort to grasp the significance of the environment in which the Bible was written, and contents itself with absolute claims about the infallible, inerrant, divine authorship of every comma and every period in the Bible. Such persons are extremely poorly informed on how the Bible, with its rich and powerful message, came to us. Preachers with such a limitation are dangerously dogmatic and deprive their listeners of the most reliable insights into religious truth.

When I began graduate study in religion more than forty years ago, I had emerged from a traumatic experience in my seminary training. I had a small congregation to serve in Providence, Rhode Island. My wife and I had been married only a year, and on the surface, things were looking promising. But after three years of merciless, critical, and historical study and the documentary approach to the Scriptures, my biblical understanding was in shambles and my theology was a mosaic of unrelated, incoherent, pious slogans.

I had been struggling for three years with a professor who was brutal in his assault upon our homegrown, simple, elementary acceptance of the Scriptures as inerrant, infallible, and divinely inspired. On the first day of class he announced that we could not be certain of anything written about Jesus except one phrase from Luke, ". . . and the child grew. . . ." As we left class, Woodrow Hasty from Wake Forest looked at me and said, "Sam, I feel like Mary at the tomb on Easter morning. They have taken away my Lord and I know not where they have laid him!"

The problem was that I had respect for the scholars who were familiar with the original languages in which the Bible was written and the cognate languages of the day—Syriac, Sumerian, Hebrew, Greek, Aramaic, Egyptian, and so forth. Moreover, these scholars were all familiar with the original manuscripts, having worked with them in museums in London and Jerusalem. They knew the geography of the area in which the Bible scenes and events were experienced. They knew also the religions and cultures that were parallel to the people who were the subjects of the Bible narratives. They had familiarity with archaeological discoveries, the tombs, the pots, the tablets, the tools, the temples and the shrines.

These scholars, equipped with such knowledge, approached our Bible and proceeded to check the accuracy of historical references and the chronology of all of the headings and sections of the writings. Their results were often in conflict with traditional beliefs, so our understanding of some of the writings had to be changed. And it took some searching and reflection to remember that God remained in place. There was a God before there was a Bible, and Jesus' saving work was done before the New Testament was written.

For a year at Yale I grappled with these issues in 125 Hopkins House. That little room became my burning bush where I had a second call to preach; it was my temple where the cherubim and seraphim visited my trembling soul and where, figuratively, a coal from the altar was placed on my tongue. It became my Damascus Road where my day was brightened by the noontide sun.

It was Harry Emerson Fosdick who towed me safely through the churning waters of my seminary days. I clung to his books, and I raced to my radio every Sunday afternoon to be there when he began, "Behold, I stand at the door and knock; saith the Lord." And with my faith lying like scraps on the floor, I stuck with him as he guided me in picking up the pieces, bit by bit, and organizing a belief system once again with joy and sweet surrender. And at Yale, I tested it all with Professor Richard Niebuhr, Liston Pope, Robert Calhoun, Julian Hart, and with the inimitable Roland Bainton.

Fosdick helped me to discover that *there was a God before there ever was a Bible* and that the same God about whom the Bible was written was the God of chemistry, pharmacology, astronomy, music, mathematics, physics, agriculture, psychology, medicine, philosophy, and all history. And that the same God still lives and throttles and monitors human affairs. So, while the Bible bore the revelation of God to us, God's existence neither began nor ended with the record in our hands. Moreover, *Jesus had been active in Judea, Samaria, Perea, and Galilee long before anyone wrote a line about him.*

The New Testament did not create Jesus; he had lived, died, and was resurrected before the New Testament began to be written. And *the church was alive and empowered by the Holy Spirit before Luke wrote a line about it.*

In other words, I was led to the same marvelous experience of the presence of the living God that caused the Old Testament to be written and into a fraternity with Jesus that transcended all other definitions of my life. A fresh awareness of the nearness of God made it clear to me why a *new name* was needed for this *new experience* called the *Holy Spirit.*

Then I had something to preach about. No longer did I need to parrot neat lines from this great "divine" or that. When preaching time came, I waited until a *sentence* was planted in my mind, one that warmed my heart and cried out to be preached. Without failing, such a *sentence*—if it came from God—could be matched by a passage somewhere in the Scriptures. Or if a verse of Scripture grabbed me first, I let it simmer until it was witnessed to by a proposition from my own faith experience that gave me the *license* to preach on it.

The Discovery of a Preaching Method

This brought me to the *dialectical* method of sermon writing. After getting the content of my faith organized, I then had to revise my sermon delivery. First, a live proposition—a divine word—that arose from Bible study, from prayer, or from an illumination that God provided in my experience, was nailed down. It had to be a sentence that stated *what I should have said by the time I had finished my sermon.*

Then I searched for the reason I had to preach on *that* proposition. And there was always a reason for preaching a certain theme; an *antithesis* waited to be exposed and laid out before the people—a condition that needed to be changed, an error in public circulation that needed to be corrected, a mood of despair that had to be dissipated, a sin that called for repentance, a dullness of spirit that needed the water of life, or a hunger for righteousness waiting for the living bread. My proposition was the answer to such an *antithesis,* and when it was clear to me, I *enlarged* the proposition into my *thesis.*

By now my Bible was back intact with a clearer understanding and a new chronology. The Pentateuch had many authors, not one; there were three Isaiahs, not one; and there could have been five letters to Corinth, not two. Jonah, Ruth, Job, and Esther could have been messages sent from God, in a literary form available and used at the time, rather than a videotape of historical events. I could deal with all of that because God was back in charge of the world, Jesus was the Lord of my life, and the Holy Spirit, the presence of God, was closer than breathing and nearer than hands and feet. I was no longer afraid of Paul's question "How shall they hear?" What are they listening for in a sermon? I write now to offer my summary of the most salient preaching propositions that have come out of this spiritual winnowing of the past forty-five years.

I have found four themes that drive my preaching like strong, moving pistons, and when I canvass the *antitheses* to these four main theses, I cannot find enough time or places to preach the sermons that are generated. These main theses are:

1. God is still present and active in human affairs and intervenes in our behalf.
2. Spiritual renewal and moral wholeness are available to us all.
3. Genuine community is a realizable goal for the human family.
4. Eternity moves through time, and immortality is an ever-present potential. We have already passed from death unto life when we love.

The title *How Shall They Hear?* comes from Romans 10:14. It is intended to signify that the preacher has an implicit contract with those who hear. We have institutionalized the preaching moment at a set time of the day on a certain day of the week in a certain place and for a certain length of time. We are far removed from the circumstances of Jeremiah, John the Baptist, or Barnabas and Paul. We are licensed, ordained, set apart, salaried, insured, and certified. Yet, despite today's formal and external canons, our purpose and function remain distinctly the same: to declare the Good News of God with relevance and conviction.

What, therefore, do the hearers expect of a sermon, week after week, from the same person, in the same place, perhaps for twenty to thirty years? What do they listen for in a sermon? What do we call success in this weekly dialogue, this celebration, this spiritual and moral engagement of minds and hearts together?

My proposal is that the four principal faith propositions dealt with in these chapters represent the core of what we should listen for in a sermon. There may be much more offered, but these (in my view) are the *sine qua non*, the basic messages that hearers are listening for from the preacher.

During those four novice years at Providence, I grew to understand that there was no more important task to be performed in the world than that of attempting to lead persons into a knowledge and understanding of spiritual reality. The preacher's task undergirds all other tasks in life, for without a binding and integrating religious perspective and conviction, all other aspects of life would be poorly aligned. And with an incomplete, fragmented, or distorted view of reality, spiritual life could be spent in dead-end pursuits, with a total waste of human capacity.

After that sojourn in Rhode Island, in fellowship with some of the finest ministers one could ever wish to know, I submerged my life (in 1949) in a forty-year involvement—teaching in colleges and universities, serving our government briefly in the Peace Corps, being the pastor of a large, vibrant urban congregation, and pursuing a vigorous extramural career preaching and lecturing in every corner of our country and many other parts of the world.

The joy I found has been unspeakable. With temerity I have carried my four main faith propositions into small rural churches in Virginia and North Carolina;

into pastors' conferences in Ohio, New Jersey, New York, Virginia, South Carolina, Georgia, Florida, California, and the Bahamas; into the chapels of our black citadels of learning—Howard, Morehouse, Lincoln, Dillard, Fisk, Hampton, Oakwood, Stilman, Virginia Union, Spelman, North Carolina A & T, Tuskegee, and countless others; from one magnificent university chapel to another—Yale, Harvard, Princeton, Columbia, Stanford, Cornell, Penn State, Bucknell, Dartmouth, Boston, Duke, Richmond, Davidson, Vanderbilt, Chicago, Emory, and Northwestern, and to many rare places of worship, including Riverside Church. It never occurred to me that I should blush to speak in the name of the Lord and challenge the best minds to consider their belief system and the coherence of their faith.

More particularly, the greatest joy has come with those for whom I had a sacred trust, the people of the Abyssinian Baptist Church in Harlem. From 1972 to 1989 I had the honor of serving as the senior minister, the person entrusted with the preaching responsibility. In our congregation was the broadest possible diversity, some persons with Ph.D's, law, and medical degrees and others with a fourth-grade education. Yet Sunday after Sunday I had the privilege of engaging the minds and hearts of that diverse group with my four fundamental questions:

1. Is God alive, aware, and active, and is God willing and able to intervene on our behalf? Is the universe a friendly place?
2. Can this carnal package of drives and urges be controlled, restrained, and reconciled to the will of God?
3. Is a blessed, genuine community possible?
4. Is our space-time frame of reference the only one, or is eternity moving through time?

An extra dividend is that in my retirement I am able to deal with all of this with ministerial students at Vanderbilt, Virginia Union, and the United Theological Seminary in Ohio.

In the following chapters I have attempted to search my mind and soul, explaining why I believe these propositions are true and why I bet my life that they are.

The assumptions the preacher may make about those who listen to sermons in today's setting are far different from the assumptions that he or she might have made one or two generations ago, in my youth, for example. I grew up in a world in which planet Earth was acknowledged to be the central, main object in the whole solar system, the principal target of the rays of the sun, brightened each night by a canopy of stars and a smiling silver moon. That any human would ever walk on that moon was in the realm of pure fantasy. Television was in the experimental stage, along with x-rays and air travel. Most people went to church; the Bible was the unquestioned, infallible word of God. Heaven had streets, rivers, and trees—a very real, physical abode. The preacher was an unquestioned authority figure in town.

In fifty years I saw all of this challenged by science, technology, and urbanization. I saw college chapels closed or virtually emptied; I watched the television medium inundate the culture. I observed so-called "healers," the "single-issue" crusaders, the "quick-fix" evangelists, and the various glib, money-grabbing assortments of anti-intellectual messiahs, adorned impeccably in sartorial splendor with gold dripping from every appendage. In the face of this I realized that listeners' worlds were shaped by the cumulus of new knowledge, that they were conditioned by the habits of reflective thought, and that they had become accustomed to honest inquiry. I recognized that there was a new audience facing the preacher of the gospel today.

Nevertheless, the challenge that the preachers face today in addressing persons influenced by scientism, secularism, and materialism is no less serious than the challenge faced by the church at many previous moments of crisis and change. No doubt, for example, the apostle Paul was pushed to his limits in cutting Christianity's umbilical cord to Judaism. Polycarp, during the persecution of Emperor Trajan, rose to sublime

heights of Christian courage by choosing to die in
flames rather than deny his Christ. Irenaeus and
Athanasius must have exhausted their gifts in saving the
young church from its early conflicts and schisms. And
as Ambrose advanced from baptism to bishop *in one single week*, he must have displayed a level of spiritual and
administrative genius that the church found indispensable in resisting the incursions by Empress Justina and
Emperor Theodosius I. Although these epochal challenges to God's servants have existed throughout the
ages, the church has prevailed.

It took an Augustine in the fifth century to reconcile
the dual claims of state and church; it took an Aquinas, a
brilliant thirteenth-century Dominican friar, to appropriate the work of the Arabic scholars of the so-called
Dark Ages and to put the thought of Aristotle to the service of Christian theology; and it took a Roman Catholic
monk, the son of a copper miner, Martin Luther, to challenge papal corruption and the vulgar excesses of Vatican authority in the sixteenth century. Black preachers
like Richard Allen and Absalom Jones in the nineteenth
century called the church to renounce its easy and comfortable accommodation to racism and to reclaim the
spirit of deliverance and inclusiveness that Jesus embraced.

Today preachers are called upon to bring their gifts
of understanding, imagination, scholarship, analysis,
and interpretation to the service of the Christian gospel
in our time and to ask the question that Paul asked in
Romans 10:14: ". . . and how shall they hear . . . ?"

The gospel deserves a fair hearing in our time, and
the human condition that we witness deserves to hear
the gospel. Today's preachers are required to define, to
declare, and to defend the gospel in the twentieth and
twenty-first centuries with the same relevance, zeal, and
commitment that Paul, Ambrose, Augustine, Aquinas,
Luther, and Richard Allen brought to their times.

The nature of the crisis of our time is well known.
The great powers of our world have been spending $600
billion a year on weaponry, while millions of lives, with-

ered from a lifetime of starving, die almost unnoticed. In South Africa the free world has allowed a contemptible denial of human decency to continue year after year with an out-gunned black majority denied the basic right of government by the consent of the governed. Small farmers in Central and South America find the production of cocaine as the only alternative to extinction; and from North America boatloads of profitable chemicals are shipped without restraint to meet the production needs of South American cocaine cartels.

In our own country the dehumanizing conditions of our inner cities have created an atmosphere in which the destruction of unemployed and undereducated young people at the hands of dope merchants goes on practically unabated. There is no effective plan for aged indigents who are chronically ill and none for unparented children who live in the streets until they are eligible for jail. The wholesale cheating of the government by big-name corporations is treated as respectable. Public officials in a long procession have had to serve prison terms, and many have ended up rich from publishing their memoirs. Racism is a major problem in our most selective centers of higher education. Narcissism and sexual permissiveness pervade the culture, fed daily and nightly by commercial television. The unrestrained idolatry of the rich is symbolized by that profane multi-million-dollar birthday party given in Morocco in September of 1989, when eight hundred of America's richest persons jetted across the ocean to eat and drink sumptuously, surrounded by and waited on by destitute people whose average per capita income was fifty dollars a month. Such are the dominant themes of our society. Most importantly, we are taught by all of the above to get rich by any means possible, and our young people believe it. This is the atmosphere in which the gospel of the Son of God must be preached. How shall they hear?

This challenge does not require the rewriting of the gospel or the redrafting of the history of the witness for Christ in the world. What it does call for is a delivery system, a relevant, coherent, convincing statement of

those salient articles of Christian belief that lifts
people out of the husks of cultural accretions and
salvages them from the accumulation of dated metaphors, from words that have lost their timbre and
phrases that have been flattened by the emptiness of
habit and superficiality.

The saddest aspect of Jimmy Baker and Jim Swag-
gart was that they could repeat the litanies of funda-
mentalism with such sweet rhythm and give the "saints"
such a soothing of the spirit with holy talk. Millions of
listeners and tens of millions of dollars were committed
to them while they lived lavishly, as they embarrassed
the calling of Christlike simplicity, sincerity, and trust.
They laquered the gospel with a varnish of pious rhetoric and emotional pretense that made "ordinary"
preachers look like novices.

What should be the response to this challenge to the
preacher today? How shall they hear? What should the
people be listening for in a sermon? They should be listening for the resonating of these major faith propositions and their application in all of the interstices and
corners of life. Moreover, when these propositions are
the preachers' very own, and when the preachers state
their basic faith propositions in *their own* language,
they preach with greater assurance and confidence;
they are far less inclined to become pablumized ver-
sions of someone else.

In the next four chapters I wish to present what I
consider to be primary faith propositions, those strong
arrows from the preacher's quiver. I would like to pro-
pose the four that I believe are waiting for an adequate
delivery system, a kind of *theology of preaching* for our
generation.

1. First, basic to the Christian belief system is the un-
    derstanding of God as absolute, wholly "other," yet
    present, participating, and aware of the details of
    all creation, history, and human endeavor, and who
    can and does intervene on our behalf in the affairs
    of the world.

2. Second, it is also basic to our faith that human nature can be renewed; we can be born again and become new creatures.
3. Third, is the conviction that, dismal and remote as it may seem at the moment, the human family can become a genuine community.
4. Fourth, also basic is the belief that our earthbound existence, our mundaneness, is given meaning and purpose by the dimension of eternity that is the ever-present potential in our midst. Immortality begins now; eternity flows in the midst of time.

What could be more magnetizing, a more luring priority, a stronger motive than to be engaged in the search for every metaphor, every analogy, every image to convey to our time the saving, the healing, the restoring, the edifying power of such good news of God?

I can hear the words of the Epistle to the Hebrews echoing now:

Wherefore seeing we also are compassed about with so great a cloud of witnesses, let us lay aside every weight, and the sin which doth so easily beset us, and let us run with patience the race that is set before us (Hebrews 12:1).

TWO

The Celebration of God's Presence and Participation in Human Affairs

Let us now examine the faith proposition that is the first arrow in the preacher's quiver—belief in God who is present and who participates in human affairs. A very few months ago we were receiving photographs of the planet Neptune, four billion miles away from planet Earth, sent by a spaceship called Voyager II that was launched twelve years ago! Such an engineering and astronomical miracle signifies the extent to which we have mastered applied mathematics, nuclear physics, mysteries of the stratosphere, the infinity of interplanetary distances, and all the subtopics ancillary to these. Such scientific wonders as this convey a convincing message to the modern mind and tempt one to believe that given more time and more money there will be no frontiers left at all.

In the summer of 1989 my cardiologist told me that I had three coronary arteries that were clogged and that I needed a triple bypass operation. Although I knew of others who had faced such surgery, my attention focused on all the details when it was my *own* heart. The

cardiologist explained that in this operation a long
blood vessel would be taken from my leg, my sternum
would be broken, my rib cage pried open, and my main
coronary arteries and my veins tightly clamped. My
heart and lungs would be shut down while a machine
did their work; and my clogged arteries would be by-
passed with detours made from that long vessel taken
from my leg. Then, after the operation, my heart and
lungs would be revitalized, the clamps removed, the
blood allowed to flow through the three new detours,
my sternum wired firmly in place, my leg stapled together . . . and life would go on. I agreed, the doctors did
the operation, and here I am. Such wonders are routine
in medicine. Again, we get the impression that, in time,
all of life's mysteries will become textbook material.
This seems like a "cause and effect" world without room
for interference by God.

Ever since the seventeenth century and the explo-
sive development in scientific thought led by Johannes
Kepler, Galileo, William Harvey, Isaac Newton, and
René Descartes (a movement given its strong impetus by
a book written by Copernicus and published while he
was dying), there has been a steady unrelenting search
for order, consistency, and predictability in the natural
world. Nowhere has this penetration into nature's secrets been more dramatic than in space research and
medicine.

This is the kind of world view, the *Zeitgeist*, the in-
tellectual environment with which the people who appear before the preacher on Sunday morning for
worship live every day. This is the world in which they
have lived Monday through Friday! They are not in
church for very long, and their expectations are high.
The preacher is not allowed to walk them through a
three-year seminary course in twenty-five minutes.
There is a finite setting, with a fixed number of minutes
available. The task is to keep alive in the hearers a faith
that gives coherence to life, that restores their broken-
ness, that draws them closer to their only source of spiritual strength. The preacher's task also is to foster a

faith that defines the hearers' moral response to their family, neighbors, nation, and the world community, a faith that gives such direction, purpose, and meaning to life that their days can be pursued with peace, joy, and meaning.

This means that the preachers must be selective in their task. If they cannot say anything helpful, what do they say? And if they fail, the consequences are clear. More and more people are denied the opportunity to hear clearly about the faith they seek, and they look elsewhere for easier, less confusing, and more palatable answers. So preachers cannot fail. By the power of God and with the guidance of the Holy Spirit, preachers must be prepared to settle on those most relevant, salient, and edifying themes of our faith and to move from one of these to another with clarity and conviction, week after week.

The people to whom the preachers minister, however, live in a world of more than technological marvels. The problems that they deal with are moral, spiritual, and emotional. They are not neat, clean-cut and symmetrical. They are amorphous, nebulous, and often filled with pain and suffering, and they hang over the hearers like slowly moving clouds. They drive them to say with the psalmist, ". . . my soul thirsteth for the living God."

The hearers are not robots; they are persons, each with his or her own unique biological make-up. Each one has his or her own package of social antecedents, genetic endowments, personality traits, and inherited values. From birth, each one begins negotiation with parents, siblings, peers, colleagues, and significant others. And in each transaction there is the potential for joy and pain, satisfaction and sorrow, fulfillment and bitter disappointment. We do not get far along this journey before we begin to reach out and start searching for a power beyond our own, for a respite, a peace, a presence in which we may find refuge, and for a protection from the worst consequences of our failures. We understand Psalm 121:

I will lift up mine eyes unto the hills, from whence cometh my
help. My help cometh from the Lord, who made heaven and earth
(Psalm 121:1–2).

It is clear that the first arrow in the preacher's
quiver, *the reality of God's presence,* is urgent, even in a
world filled with the magic of science and technology.
God is a power and a presence who is aware of our condition and who is able to intervene on our behalf.

We are also physical, fragile, and finite beings who
can be burdened beyond our strength and taxed beyond
our power to cope. We are created, derivative beings
with limits, and life will drag every one of us to his or
her limit, time and time again. We invest our trust in
others who betray us. In quest of some of our most cov-
eted prizes we find the competition too formidable, and
we are embarrassingly outranked. We often stumble before strong temptations and never cease to pay a price
that we never imagined. We take a risk on the choice of a
career, a partner in marriage, and in rearing a family,
and success at any or all of these can be shaky and tenuous at best. Sharing our lives with others who need us
can deplete our means and our strength; extended ill-
nesses that we feel we never deserved can cling like a
pall; and besides all of this, we are still random candi-
dates for street violence, airplane crashes, violent
storms, war casualties, freak accidents, and mental
breakdowns.

So, when the preacher enters the pulpit, the hearers
are physical, finite beings among whom there is a random distribution of all the conditions previously
named. When the preacher begins to preach, the hearers
begin to listen for some word that assures them that
they are not alone in this world. They will not be surprised at all to hear the preacher say out of the depths of
her or his own soul, reflecting the preacher's felt need:

God is our refuge and strength, a very present help in trouble.
Therefore will not we fear, though the earth be removed, and
though the mountains be carried into the midst of the sea . . . The

LORD of hosts is with us; the God of Jacob is our refuge (Psalm 46:1,2,7).

Those who await the messages are also members of a society with certain customs and norms and with institutions that bear the public trust. In a sense they have investments in the well-being of that society. Persons sensitive to this relationship do care about social outcomes. They see social capital wasted on the drug scourge, millions of undereducated and oppressed persons living with total dependency on public funds, persons in high positions brought to disgrace for malfeasance, and poverty clinging to some families for generations while politicians, entertainers, ballplayers, and stock manipulators get millions a year to spend on extravagant lifestyles. They see families falling apart and children growing up in a moral vacuum, while gnawing within them are frustration, a sense of futility, and unease about the future. All of this leads people to feel like calling on some kind of a higher power, some authority, appealing for judgment, for a voice from heaven, for an Amos out of Tekoa crying, "Let justice run down as waters, and righteousness as a mighty stream" (Amos 5:24, KJV).

Moreover, those who serve congregations of persons victimized by racism, chronic economic depression, social ostracism, and stubborn stereotypes face a task hardly known to other preachers. They will find a hunger for identity, a thirst for freedom, and a zeal for liberation that cannot be quenched with palliatives and mild bromides. Preaching for those individuals must somehow bring God very near so that they feel God's presence with ecstasy and joy. Their worship is not a forum for debate, a lyceum to consider many alternatives, but a temple where one mighty conclusion is known, felt, and celebrated. They sing:

> Glory, glory, hallelujah!
> Since I laid my burden down.
> I feel better, so much better,
> Since I laid my burden down.

Friends don't treat me like they used to,
Since I laid my burden down.
Going home, to live with Jesus,
Since I laid my burden down.[1]

So, how then shall they hear? What then should
happen when the minister preaches about faith in a God
who is aware of our situation and intervenes on our behalf? What should the hearers expect?

A Coherent View of the World

First of all, if the hearers are to affirm faith in a God
who is active and involved and whose finger is on the
pulse of our times, they must have a functional, coherent view of the world. Everyone really needs some kind
of an operational view of the world, *some sense of the
ultimate.*

No doubt the ministers will preach to some who
have debated for a long time about the details of the
world and who have deferred indefinitely their conclu-
sions about God. One may try to go about living with a
big question mark hanging over the whole "God" idea; in
fact, many *are* trying to do just that. But no one goes on
successfully for very long without some kind of a work-
able God idea, some grand hypothesis about the ultimate meaning of life. Most persons do have one, but they
may not have ever written it down on paper or confessed
it to anyone. No doubt there is something that all of us
who cope with life say to ourselves every morning,
either in quiet, tacit consent or in a hymn that we hum
or in a prayer that we mumble to ourselves. We put some
kind of a *sign* up every day about how we view the world,
whether it is well conceived or not.

And, my friends, the most honorable calling in life
is the call to surrender oneself in the service of helping
persons to find that *best sign* to put up, the best working

---

[1]"Glory, Glory, Hallelujah," traditional spiritual.

premise about life, that best early-morning faith proposition that most adequately accounts for the total human experience. When preachers let that first arrow fly
from their quivers, they are affirming with the people
what the psalmist sang so beautifully, helping them to
find spiritual coherence and meaning:

> The earth is the LORD's and the fullness thereof, the world, and
> they that dwell therein. For he hath founded it upon the seas, and
> established it upon the floods. Who shall ascend into the hill of
> the LORD? or who shall stand in his holy place? He that hath clean
> hands, and a pure heart; who hath not lifted up his soul unto van-
> ity, nor sworn deceitfully. He shall receive the blessing from the
> LORD, and righteousness from the God of his salvation (Psalm
> 24:1–5).

The widespread use of narcotics and hallucinogens
may be telling us something about the lack of an intel-
lectually coherent and spiritually satisfying world view
in our society. It is frightening to observe how many persons there are in our society who have a chemical depen-
dence on such drugs as alcohol, cocaine, "crack," or
addictive prescription drugs.

Effective preaching tries to sell a view of the world
that one can live with while facing all of life's stark and
bold realities. Being left with only a cold mechanistic
world and with no more of a God than a "first cause" or
an "unmoved mover" leaves large areas of our experience unaccounted for. Our very presence in the world —
with the kind of minds we have, with the freedom we
have, with the aesthetic hunger we have, with our
boundless proclivity to create, and with our proneness
to make so much more out of life than an atavistic race
for survival — defies our settling for a world that was
only a chemical, physical, biological accident. The pre-
supposition that there is a mind behind it all, with freedom, power, and volition, who made the physical world
and who had a moral agenda for us in the world, leads to
a far more adequate answer. So the first task to accomplish through preaching is a settlement with the hearers
about a God who can and does intervene in our world

and in human affairs. Everyone needs an adequate God concept.

One day while on an airplane flight, I was involved in a long conversation about religion with a young engineering graduate from an outstanding midwestern state university. He pursued congenially one question after another until he asked this one: "When do you think the thousand years will expire and the dragon, Satan, will be loosened?" He was referring to a passage in the book of Revelation (20:1–3), a part of John's vision, and he had taken it literally. He had no idea of when or how Satan had been tied (whether with rope, stainless steel, grapevine, or chain), whether Satan ate, drank, slept, or talked with anyone, where Satan was tied, or by whom! It was pitiful to see a bright engineering graduate with such an inadequate God concept, such a weak introduction to the Bible, and with such a juvenile, foggy, and misinstructed view of the world. Imagine, he allowed himself for all those years to believe that a cosmic, physical devil was tied to a tree stump in some location around Tel Aviv, Cyprus, or Istanbul! He was feeling his way through life with a weak, inadequate, incoherent view of the world, and he needed help from a well-equipped, committed preacher.

The preacher who helps most in getting people to grasp a mature, coherent view of the world, with an adequate God idea will know the Bible well and will help people to remember that there is only one God, who is indeed Alpha and Omega, who stood on nothing and made a world before "the morning stars sang together, and all the sons of God shouted for joy" (Job 38:7). And this God is not insulted if we understand the nature of our world with all the acumen that God has given us.

Speaking of a coherent world view that derives from a well-founded faith, I visited my attorney to have my will reviewed. Open-heart surgery brings such reminders! As we closed the business conversation, he wanted, as usual, to talk with me about religion. He is a well-read Christian layman, seriously involved in his American Baptist church, and a respected attorney specializing in wills and trusts. He told me that he had spent his summer vacation in Jamaica with a group of volunteers doing masonry, plumbing, and carpentry work, building houses for the poor in that country. He paid all of his own expenses and contributed two weeks of intensive labor among Jamaica's poor. He is a suburban, Ivy League–educated lawyer whose view of the world is "together." This person has a faith that enables him to see the world with spiritual poise and well-placed faith. His conversation revealed that underneath a very active and successful law career there lay a firm commitment to a faith that overflowed into action. His world has a God behind it whom he worships as the ultimate "significant other" in his life.

This God did intervene and entered the world in Jesus Christ. Believing that, my lawyer friend found in Jesus the paradigm of a godly, fulfilled life. Following Jesus in loving obedience, my friend went to Jamaica to build houses for the poor. This is one of the outcomes that we can expect when we get across to the people an adequate God concept in Jesus Christ.

Personal Moral Commitment

A strong faith in a God who is involved in the world not only provides a coherent world view, but also provides a basis for personal moral commitment. Everyone makes decisions, and these decisions are based on a personal value system. Here again, many may not have ever announced what their value systems are or how they were put together; but if we follow these people around with a video recorder we can tell them what their value systems are. Their lives show their values!

There are many ways by which we arrive at a value system, our own way of determining what is right and what is wrong. Sadly enough, many persons simply follow what is customary, what seems like common sense, without any questioning whatsoever. Many to whom we preach do just that, and a clearer conviction about God's concern for the world should challenge such a casual approach to the good life. When we follow custom and convention, we are really deferring our moral choices to others and not making these choices ourselves. Much of racism and materialism remains with us because it is rooted in the culture, and custom holds it in place. The treatment of women as inferiors, for example, in the workplace, the home, the church, and before the law derives from long and tired customs that die hard.

Faith in God and in God's self-revelation in Jesus Christ causes moral judgments to be based on God's love of us and of all humans *equally*, with no one entitled to a privilege or subject to a limitation that *all* of us would not enjoy or suffer equally. Moreover, our moral values are further defined by the intrinsic worth and dignity of *each* life, as Jesus indicated in his ministry and in his teaching. Our moral choices are made on this basis: treat everyone as an equal with inherent worth conferred by God our Creator. From this flows a flood of moral decisions and judgments as we apply it to concrete situations. It begins with our faith in God and in the transparent illumination of the moral life in Jesus Christ.

A Haven from the Tempests of Life

Finally, when the ministers preach to the people that God is in the world with us and not a blind, heedless, impersonal force without a name who cannot hear and answer prayers, they give the people the most enduring foundation for emotional stability, spiritual poise, and the ballast and equilibrium that living requires. Augustine said that our restless souls would find no rest until we found our rest in God. The normal ranges of life's vicissitudes will keep any person looking for something to hold on to.

We need much from our faith. Our religion does not start out looking for tranquility; we need theological grounding and moral commitment first. But when these are in place, as a consequence, our religion does provide for us a haven from the tempests of life.

While preparing this material, I was kept awake and alarmed by televised reports of the devastation of a hurricane in Jamaica, Puerto Rico, and South Carolina, an earthquake in California, a tornado in Alabama, and another twister in New York that killed seven school children. Deaths mounted into the hundreds as bridges collapsed, cars were slammed against trees, roofs of buildings were blown away, and houses were washed into the seas.

I landed in San José for a conference only days after their earthquake and while some aftershocks were still rumbling. While awaiting my luggage at the carousel, I chanced to stand near a local resident, and I asked, "How are the people taking this? What is the emotional recovery rate?" She took time to think about her answer and said something to this effect:

Well, I can't speak for others, but as for me, I have space in my world for such as we have seen. I believe that if we had a quake, it was necessary and we could not have avoided it. Nature had some business to attend to. I would *like* a world without storms, floods, earthquakes, and genetic flaws; and if one were available, my faith tells me that God would surely have given it to us. So, this world that we have must be the *best world that God had!* Next, it is designed to bring out the best that is in us—faith in the face of mystery, love in the face of suffering, education and exploration in the face of ignorance, and patience, compassion, and fortitude in the face of suffering. Another thing, we are just passing through, and we die only once. If death occurs in one of these catastrophes, that was our particular farewell. Others will follow us with a different departure: stroke, heart failure, cancer, murder, drowning, or a car crash. This is a physical world, and it is only our temporary abode. In the midst of these natural physical necessities, however, God is with us to see us through.

When our preaching brings about such a result as that kind of faith, it ought to warm our hearts. How shall they hear? They need to know that there is a way of reckoning with disaster, to know that on one hand the unfailing processes of nature produce such wonders as the natural eye, design the billion cells that make the brain, set the rhythm between the heart and the lungs, and regulate the exchange of oxygen and carbon dioxide between trees and human beings, and that on the other hand all of this comes with a price—the tragic likelihood that these wonders may bring us suffering and pain when in their performance they have to yield to some hidden necessities that are still beyond our wisdom. But faith in God holds us steady and secure in all of this; in the midst of such an enigma, we believe in the goodness of God and that as the mountains are around Jerusalem, so the Lord is around us.

How shall they hear? They need desperately to be assured that, despite these catastrophes, the world is not a blind cosmic machine and that behind it is more than a chemical formula or a mathematical postulate. They need to be reminded that for every flood that nature imposes on us, a million miles of gently flowing rivers and streams keep their bounds every day; for every September hurricane, there are fifty weeks of quiet skies, gentle winds, and unannounced daybreaks that unfold without a whimper. For every tidal wave that destroys beachfront homes and washes roads away, there are billions of acres of rolling, fertile lands that yield their harvests unbegrudgingly and on which we depend with bonded assurance.

They need to hear the preacher say that in the midst of the pain we are called upon to endure, when nature strains and groans to keep its powerful forces in delicate balance, it is still God's world. It is the best world that could be made. God knows the risks that we run living in it. God is able and available to walk with us through all of this travail.

> From every stormy wind that blows,
> From every swelling tide of woes,
> There is a calm, a sure retreat;
> 'Tis found beneath the mercy seat.[2]

---

[2]"From Every Stormy Wind That Blows," by Hugh Stowell.

How shall they hear? They need to hear that God cared enough to come into our midst in the life of a carpenter's son, among ordinary people in the fullness of time, to share this earthbound abode with us, to taste our existence, our hurt, our pain, and the limitations that we endure, even the chilly hand of death and, then, to open wide the gates of heaven through the marvelous victory of Christ over death and the grave. God is with us in all of the ebb and flow of our days.

They need to be reminded that none of us came here to stay. This earthbound abode of ours is for but a season. Our ultimate purpose here is not to pursue physical comfort and solace, but to become at one with God; we must affirm this in love and with caring. This ultimate at-oneness with God is not consummated in the midst of these earthbound trappings, in this maze of compromises and half-truths in which we are groping. There is a freedom that awaits us and a never-ending day.

In my college we had a preaching club, a lyceum where ministerial students would practice preaching before the group in alphabetical order, ready or not. One student in our group suffered from muscular spasms; his head would swing from side to side uncontrollably and he walked with a cane as his knees constantly rubbed together painfully. Because of poor vision, he wore conspicuous, thick lenses. Everyone on campus helped him and showed him sympathy. Because of his genetic flaw, he lived each day with great difficulty. He was the victim of one of nature's awful embarrassments, where the DNA imprint was most imprecise. He was called upon to find the courage, the personal resilience, and the indomitable faith to live his life. We were put to shame by his gutsy daily routine. And he was poor, needing everything.

When this fellow's name came up alphabetically, it was his turn to preach. We all sat in childish curiosity, everyone wishing really that this one student could be exempted, but he seemed to want to do it. Life had dealt him his condition, and he had learned to cope with it. He began by asking us to sing a hymn with him, and without

having a book that included his hymn, he "worded" it for
us:

> On Jordan's stormy banks I stand,
> And cast a wishful eye
> To Canaan's fair and happy land,
> Where my possessions lie.
>
> No chilling winds nor pois'nous breath
> Can reach that healthful shore;
> Sickness and sorrow, pain and death
> Are felt and feared no more.
>
> I am bound for the promised land,
> I am bound for the promised land;
> O who will come and go with me?
> I am bound for the promised land.[3]

He did not need to give a sermon. By the time he finished his song of faith, he had convinced us all that from
the worst of circumstances, from his pit of agony, it is
possible to discover that God is alive, active, aware, and
able to sustain us in the total range of human conditions.

---

[3]"On Jordan's Stormy Banks I Stand," by Samuel Stennett.

THREE

The Assurance of Spiritual Renewal and Moral Wholeness

There is no music, no poetry, no gem of architecture or any achievement in technology more wonderful, more beautiful, more moving, more worth celebrating than a human life that has dealt successfully with the basic "stuff" of our carnal existence. Despite the ugliness, the cynicism, and the inhumanity that surrounds us, the preacher is called upon to lift up before the people this central theme of the gospel: Human nature can be harnessed and tamed, we can be born anew, and the mind of Christ can be in us. First and always we are of the flesh, with the most relentless drives and urges to satisfy our carnal desires. Even nature, with all of its marvels—the speed of a cheetah, the silken petals of a rose, the spread of the wings of a condor, the majesty of the silent Himalayan peaks—still fails to match an excelsior character, one who has the integrity, the consistency, the predictability of a human life that has harnessed these animal appetites and has brought them under the control of the mind of Christ. Wherever a human being has been able to integrate his or her glandular and neurological equipment and has brought the torrents of unrelenting necessities under control, we can see something of the highest order of creation.

Every preacher should carry to the pulpit this arrow in his or her quiver: the assurance that life can indeed resonate to the highest values and vibrate to the finest examples of those premier personalities that have crossed the stage of life. When the news is bad and the reports on the human condition are at their very worst, the preacher must be prepared to give the assurance again and again:

> Come now, and let us reason together, saith the LORD: though your sins be as scarlet, they shall be as white as snow; though they be red like crimson, they shall be as wool (Isaiah 1:18).

> I am come that they might have life, and that they might have it more abundantly (John 10:10).

The people need to hear it affirmed over and over:

> For the law of the Spirit of life in Christ Jesus hath made me free from the law of sin and death. For what the law could not do, in that it was weak through the flesh, God sending his own Son in the likeness of sinful flesh, and for sin, condemned sin in the flesh: That the righteousness of the law might be fulfilled in us, who walk not after the flesh, but after the Spirit (Romans 8:2–5).

The Good News of the gospel is that God knows our origin and our condition and yet, through the prophets and through the grace of Jesus Christ, we are called to walk in lofty places. The amazing message of the Bible is not so much the exposure of the depths to which humankind can sink, but the heights to which we are beckoned. Some of the sorriest characters of all time were called to unbelievable moral summits. Jacob was a talented hustler, conspiring with Rebekah, his mother, to rob his brother Isaac of his inheritance. Later when he was in deep trouble, he was helped by Laban, his uncle, but when his chance came, he was not reluctant to deceive Laban and rob him of his cattle. Yet, as the events of his checkered life unfolded, his name was changed to Israel, and he became the father of a nation. From a scheming, sly, deceptive opportunist, Jacob became the father of the twelve tribes of Israel. Moses was a fugitive in Midian, having slain an Egyptian and hidden the body in the sand, but God found Moses beside Mount Horeb and called him to deliver his people. David schemed to have Uriah slain in battle so that he could take his wife, yet after his repentance there came from his lips some of the most cherished words about the greatness and the goodness of the Lord.

Paul belonged to a band of zealots who pledged to destroy Christians. At the stoning of Stephen the mob laid their clothes at the feet of Paul, who was then called Saul. Simon Peter, Jesus' closest friend, lied under pressure and swore he never knew Jesus. But these two, Peter and Paul, described in detail for their moral lapses and their actions against Jesus, became the true heroes of the Bible, the founders of the church, faithful servants of Christ, martyrs for the gospel's sake, and the most revered names in the history of the church.

The preacher has a lot to work with when he or she sets out to show that human nature can be renewed. The record is replete with the stories of the lives of persons such as Saint Augustine, who lived a wild and reckless life before he surrendered to Christ. One of the most familiar themes in all drama, music, art, and poetry is the story of a life sunk in sin and later crowned with moral and spiritual victory, from plays by Euripides and Shakespeare to *Anna Lucasta* and *Porgy and Bess*.

One of the finest opportunities that the preacher has from the pulpit is to confront all persons with the possibilities for renewal and restoration, to begin where they are with whatever may be their degree of alienation and estrangement, and to help them find the freedom to center on Christ and experience spiritual and moral wholeness. One of the rewards of retirement is the mail that comes from the least-expected persons, expressing delayed appreciation for a sermon or a counseling session that took his or her feet out of the "mire and the clay" and set them on a rock.

Every life is dragged and threatened by the undertow of that primeval human arrogance, the hubris that prods us to take things into our own hands, to throw caution to the wind, and to "do our own thing." We all can attest to the difficulty that we face in resisting the "wiles of the devil." We all know how brief these victories are and how these temptations have to be fought on a recurring basis; we all know what Paul was referring to when he complained,

> . . . when I would do good, evil is present with me. For I delight in the law of God after the inward man: But I see another law in my members, warring against the law of my mind, and bringing me into captivity to the law of sin . . . (Romans 7:21–23).

Every Sunday morning in our solemn sanctuaries, those warriors who are engaged in this battle with our "lower nature" are made welcome. And, on this issue, how *shall* they hear? What is the good word? The assurance that they need is the promise found in the First Epistle of John:

> If we confess our sins, he is faithful and just to forgive us our sins, and to cleanse us from all unrighteousness (1 John 1:9).

> . . . greater is he that is in you, than he that is in the world (1 John 4:46).

The preacher must bring this word that we are not in a losing battle and that renewal, restoration, and redemption are possible and available.

The Bible is filled with metaphors and symbols that stand for the evil that is pervasive in the world. While Judaism embraced the strongest witness to the one God whose name was Jehovah, it was difficult to lose the notion that somehow Satan—a name and a person with demonic powers, agents, and subordinates—was loose in the world. Our proneness to evil was easily assigned to Satan. Indeed, today we have no less evil in our world, but we are not willing to accept the confusion that follows when we fill the world with demons and a "chief devil."

The realities for which such labels stood are still with us, but they need new names and new labels to be understood by people today. The point is, whether there are demons and a devil or not, the struggle is just as formidable. The preacher must bring the assurance that Jesus did not come into the world in vain. He did not call us to spiritual and moral maturity to tease us. He came in earnest, and when he said, "Follow me," he meant that it was possible. When he said, "Blessed are the pure in heart," it meant that our hearts could become pure.

Notwithstanding the sublime heights to which Christ calls us and the possibility of our redemption, when we read the morning paper and hear the evening news on television, it appears that this redemption is farfetched and illusory. It seems that every sin in Paul's inventory from Galatians 5 is found among us in magnified proportions: "adultery, fornication, uncleanness, lasciviousness, idolatry, witchcraft, hatred, variance, emulations, wrath, strife, seditions, heresies, envyings, murders, drunkenness, revellings, and such like . . ." (Galatians 5:19–21). Whatever was attributed to the devil and his aides has remained with us in our generation and resounds in our midst in octaves.

As created beings we are endowed with our own survival propensities. Everything that grows and creeps on the face of the earth and everything that inhabits the briny seas fights to survive. Beavers build dams, skunks exude odors, octopuses spray inks and dyes, chameleons change colors, oysters grow shells, and birds hide eggs in order to help them to survive. And when we turn to the *Homo sapiens* with the big brains, the tool-making thumbs, verbs that are conjugated, and the past perfect tense used in grammar, we will find every conceivable trick to promote survival. In actual practice such tricks turn out to be a drive for security, an ego projection for recognition, a fierce competitiveness for an advantage, racism for group superiority, along with common greed,

cheating, stealing, and payroll padding. The demons
may have other names, but they are here! The preacher
needs to point them out to the people so they can be recognized and so the nature of the struggle can be understood.

There are explanations for the origin of what turns
out to be sin and evil in our lives. We are equipped for
reproduction, for example, and around this gift many
demons gather. We have tried to give sanctity and dignity to reproduction by instituting the monogamous
marriage; we have tried to enhance the development of
our children by establishing the home, the "nest," the in-
cubator. But at the center of all of this is that powerful
reproductive endowment with its uncontrollable urges.
We try to sublimate these with all sorts of art forms and
deflective exercises like dancing, but the "demons" keep
appearing.

We have tried to organize orderly ways for humans
to protect self-interest in all sorts of mutual and partici-
patory ways, culminating in the creation of the state,
with statutory governments. But the "demons" appear
again, seeking control, promoting class and racial strife,
colonizing and enslaving others, and making endless
war.

The net result is that our sheer creatureliness generates possibilities for all kinds of moral failure. One
wonders how the young manage to grow up as sane as
they are in the moral confusion that they witness. Corporations with time-honored names and reputations are
paying the government huge fines for cheating on defense contracts; Ivy League alumni are carted off to
prison for fraud in the stock market, while already earn-
ing millions a year; professional athletes, the idols of the
nation's youth, are fined constantly for drug abuse and
jailed frequently for immoral acts.

It is clear that the word could easily spread that human nature is hopelessly polluted. The role of the
preacher becomes more and more distinct. The need for
this arrow in the quiver becomes imperative. How shall
they hear? What are they listening for? We patiently

await some word that assures us that earnestness in trying to please God will not be in vain.

> For as the rain cometh down, and the snow from heaven, and re-
> turneth not thither, but watereth the earth, and maketh it bring
> forth and bud, that it may give seed to the sower, and bread to the
> eater: So shall my word be that goeth forth out of my mouth: it
> shall not return unto me void, but it shall accomplish that which I
> please, and it shall prosper in the thing whereto I sent it" (Isaiah
> 55:10–11).

God has set *Homo sapiens* on planet Earth, "made a
little lower than the angels, and crowned with glory and
honor." From our finite perspective we cannot decipher
all of the mysteries of God's purposes. Nevertheless, the
panting within us tells us that we thirst for the living
God. Like Thompson's "hound of heaven,"[1] with unhurry-
ing but unbroken pace, God has pursued us. It is the
preacher's burden to assure the people that we are not
meant to linger at the swine's trough in a strange land,
but to head home to our father's house and to find him in
the road, watching every silhouette that parts the curtain of darkness, with a new ring for our finger and a
new robe to drape on our drooping shoulders. Human
nature can be restored, renewed, reclaimed, and redeemed.

There are sound foundations for this conviction.
For one thing, despite the tendency toward evil, the tendency toward good is always around also. The first clue
to higher possibilities is this: While we may understand
and acknowledge this proneness toward evil that em-
barrasses us in every generation—this carnal, animal
nature that is so hard to harness—where does this prodding toward *goodness* come from, this selfless love of
which we are so capable, this compassion that is so enduring and that will not spend itself? What is the source
of this motivation to do good that stays in tension with
the undertow that drags us on toward evil?

---

[1]See Francis Thompson, *The Hound of Heaven* (various publishers).

During the 1989 assault of Hurricane Hugo on Charleston, South Carolina, reports came from that ravaged region that gasoline stations were gouging their neighbors with a price of $4.50 for a gallon of gas. Ice plants were selling ice at $10 a bag. The National Guard had to patrol the streets to keep pilferers from hauling off their neighbors' furniture and groceries. This kind of behavior is traceable to that unredeemed carnality— raw, survival propensities unchanneled by higher values or by the mind and Spirit of Christ. On the other hand, a convoy of fourteen-wheel trucks loaded with food had already begun rolling to Charleston from Lancaster, Pennsylvania; Roanoke, Virginia; Charlotte, North Carolina; Trenton, New Jersey; Hartford, Connecticut; Long Island, New York; Brunswick, Georgia; and Miami, Florida. The Red Cross and the Salvation Army reported cash flowing in. Can human nature be redeemed? From somewhere there rises within us a summons to shake free of the fetters that bind us to our carnal nature so that we can soar toward our higher nature.

At our church some time ago, we began to receive rather frequent and sizable contributions with no name or address given. We assumed that it was from a modest person who preferred simply not to be acknowledged. After a while these gifts began to total a rather large sum, so we became apprehensive about the source. One day a Harlem drug dealer came to my study with expensive jewelry on each wrist and pure gold swinging from his neck; he wore "mod" boots, designer jeans and jacket, and a huge diamond ring sparkling with opulence. He was that anonymous donor of generous sums to the church, and finally he showed up to identify himself and to tell me how uncomfortable he was with all of that poison money. Incidentally, in the meantime a relative of his had called the church to ask if, on the basis of his gifts, we would write a character reference for him to help him with a plea bargain on a drug-pushing indictment! Of course, we could not and did not. Had one seen him cruising the streets in his big black sedan with smoked windows, one might have concluded that the demons had full possession of him. One would hardly have thought that he was trying to find the courage to slip into the church to confess his wrong and to cry unashamedly before the preacher about the vulgar, dangerous, and useless life he had lived.

Indeed, evil is a problem and demons are a problem. But our problem is, also, what was it that caused the drug dealer to feel so wasted and incomplete? What was it that kept me awake all night at age seventeen, got me up early one Sunday morning in Williams Hall at Virginia State College, and made me go to the Zion Baptist Church and sit still until Reverend J. B. Brown told me what God had planted in his heart to say to the people?

Generation after generation we see new waves of evil deeds and thoughts surging like a heavy tide upon the human scene. Just as surely, human nature counters with a responding tide of simple good will. This tells us that we cannot escape. We will never be left at ease wallowing in our sin. We will always be haunted by the sentiments of William Cowper's familiar lines:

> Where is the blessedness I knew
> When first I saw the Lord?
> Where is the soul-refreshing view
> Of Jesus and His word?
>
> Return, O Holy Dove, return
> Sweet Messenger of rest;
> I hate the sins that made Thee mourn,
> And drove Thee from my breast."[2]

Next, consider that even though evil abounds, our full potential is best realized when we are pursuing good and not evil, nurturing life rather than dealing death, building community rather than estrangement. There is no way to account for our total natural, marvelous, human endowments and capacities unless we are investing them in the pursuit of human good. The evil

---

[2]"O for a Closer Walk with God," by William Cowper.

that lures us does not utilize our total capacity. When we finish sinning, much of our talent and ability is unaccounted for, like a car moving in reverse all the time and leaving four forward gears waiting to be engaged for forward movement!

When I learned that certain New Jersey state policemen were stealing cocaine from a locked storage closet, a closet that held court evidence, and were planting it on black motorists who had been stopped and harassed on the New Jersey Turnpike, I thought of what a perverted use of authority and police training that was. And when they were caught, fired, and held for conviction, embarrassing their families and other decent troopers, I thought of how much talent and high ability had gone to waste, what a loss of time in prison, and what a cynical report to give the drug merchants. We are equipped to do better things with our genius; this equipment cannot be fully accounted for in doing dirty tricks to one another. South Africa has much more to give to the world than an archaic, disingenuous system of racial subjugation. When that country is finally awakened from this nightmare, the world will be stunned to see what this potent phoenix of the ocean really can produce, how the desert will bloom and the dormancy of a long-abused continent will flower in full fecundity. In our own South, in Atlanta, Birmingham, Columbia, Durham, Greensboro, Norfolk, Nashville, Roanoke, and Fredericksburg there is a vibrancy, a propensity, a surge of growth after the anesthesia of rigid racial segregation has finally worn off.

When the industrial nations of the world exploit the poverty-smitten peoples of the less developed countries by selling them cancer-causing cigarettes, polluting their air with unregulated chemical manufacturing, poisoning their fishing waters with experimental nuclear explosions, selling them the chemicals necessary for cocaine production, and employing them at rock-bottom wages, this may seem smart and good business. But it causes four of the five billion people of the world to hate us, it causes our children to inherit a polarized and bellicose world political environment, it creates wars and violence, it erodes our highest values, and it is not the best use of our brains.

A better use would be to find ways to help those four billion to develop economies that would enhance the quality of their lives consonant with their culture and traditions, to promote education and a trained work force, to reduce the negative consequences of generations of colonialism, to discover agricultural breakthroughs that would feed and nurture the world's hungriest people, and to share our medical marvels with the sickest and weakest people on the planet. We have that ability, and it is disengaged too generally. Such latent talent and such ideas lying fallow do signify to us, however, that we were equipped for something better than plunder, exploitation, military domination, and alienation.

One of the sad facts of our time is that so many of our fine young minds have been lured into careers in big business, with the promise of quick riches and early retirement to a golf course and a white, sandy beach. Students are lined up at the opening of every semester for courses that teach how the market works and how it can be manipulated. Of course, profits must be made to create jobs, to pay taxes, to keep an economy vital, but there are very few chaplains and counselors around who bring another offering to students' attention. It is all so one-sided. Rumors of high earnings are irresistible, and the commitment to the cult of money is firm. Also, for the past ten years the country has promoted a kind of national cult of things and wealth. Taxes for the well-off were cut; contempt for the poor became common; a "trickle-down" economic policy prevailed; deregulation set heavy financial speculation in motion; corporate takeovers, quick junk-bond sales, and the pilfering of government programs such as housing for the poor by the power brokers set the tone.

The net result is that many of the best minds are crowded into the fields of engineering, computer science, and schools of business. We need some of them to

enter fields that will help house the homeless, manage
the nation's health care, educate our underprivileged,
and develop a foreign policy that includes something
new and different to aid less developed nations in im-
proving their quality of life. This will engage our finest
minds to the fullest. We are designed and created for
heavy assignments in doing good!

A young man sneaking through the darkness of an
urban ghetto, dropping off crack to make five hundred
dollars in a night, and ending up in jail for twelve years
has no idea of what his true abilities are. I saw the
leader of a hate group on television recently parroting
unscientific lies about racial groups and trying to fo-
ment a national antiblack, anti-Jewish movement. His
ideas, his language, all his efforts were juvenile and pal-
pably simple-minded, although treacherous. I wondered what he would be if, for God's sake, he turned
around and began to explore the talent that his genes
held latent and inert within him.

The possibilities within us for goodness and greatness are a basis for believing that human nature was not
meant to be a total investment in evil. We are equipped
to heal diseases, to educate the illiterate, to counsel the
wayward, to feed the hungry, to build real community,
to protect the environment, to develop faltering economies, to stimulate production, to write poems and sym-
phonies, to identify the farthest star, to care for
abandoned babies, and to provide for the weak and the
powerless. If we fail in these things, we allow this wealth
of human capacity that God gave us to lie fallow. From
the earliest of times we have known that the freedom to
choose good over evil was a basic human attribute:

> I call heaven and earth to record this day against you, that I have
> set before you life and death, blessing and cursing: therefore,
> choose life, that both thou and thy seed may live . . .
> (Deuteronomy 30:19).

The third foundation for our faith in the achievement of moral wholeness is what we observe not only in
our personal spiritual quest or in the unused capacity

for good that we possess, but in what we observe in the long sweep of history. Indeed, it often does appear that life is a "tale told by an idiot signifying nothing," but that is the short-range view of things. The long-range view is what James Russell Lowell concluded in the poem "The Present Crisis":

> Truth forever on the scaffold, Wrong for-
> ever on the throne, –
> Yet that scaffold sways the future, and be-
> hind the dim unknown
> Standeth God within the shadow, keeping
> watch above his own.

I have a class of college freshmen and sophomores who were not born when Martin Luther King, Jr., was shot to death in Memphis in April 1968. They did not know the world of my youth. They know only of the civil rights changes, the world of Nixon, Carter, Reagan, and Bush. The only Supreme Court they know is the one stacked against affirmative action. They know the Harlem and the Newark of the drug kings, the rat-infested, worn-out tenements, families without fathers, and police shooting teenage blacks and Puerto Ricans. That world is real enough, but they do not know how long colonialism lasted and what it took to dismantle that world where barefooted, illiterate coolies worked endless hours for a bowl of rice and where carefully selected governors-general, appointed by the king, served in black colonies. These young students never saw the world of "colored" toilets at the back of filling stations or balconies for blacks in theaters everywhere. They did not know the world when blacks were not admitted to Columbia, Rutgers, the University of Pennsylvania, and Princeton except with special presidential action, and when blacks could not enter Duke, Virginia, Georgia Tech, Clemson, Baylor, or Vanderbilt with anyone's consent!

The present condition of women, blacks, the poor, the aged, and the indigent chronically ill is in many respects still deplorable and calls for change. That is one

set of facts. Another set of facts includes the origins of
these present conditions, the resistance to change that
they met, and the irresistible and persistent pressures
that caused them to be where they are now. We did not
always have a black chairman of the Joint Chiefs of
Staff. For generations we had segregated military units
with no black commissioned officers at all. We did not
always have a black quarterback winning a Super Bowl.
For the longest time no blacks could play professional
ball at all. We did not always have two American League
finalists in the baseball playoffs that each had a black
manager. Last year a baseball executive was *fired* for
saying that blacks were built for speed and strength but
not for thinking and managing.

When I read in Genesis that Abraham, Isaac, and Jacob had their hundreds of manservants and maidser-
vants trekking across the desert behind the goats, the
sheep, and the camels, and that they used women and
children like property, I appreciate what a long way we
have come and the degree to which human nature has
adjusted to a revised view of personhood.

We don't know what will come of it, but we have
been witnessing the heads of the Soviet Union and the
United States arranging for the destruction of chemical
war materials. Recently the chief of Russia's military
visited Fort Bragg, North Carolina, where our shock
troops are trained, where the paratroopers learn to drop
behind enemy lines. All of this looks very strange to one
who has lived through three wars. The crumbling of the
Berlin Wall, the cry for freedom in Eastern Europe and
China, and the turning of the worm in South Africa signify a force still alive in history, a moving toward freedom reminiscent of the end of the divine right of kings,
the beginning of government by the governed, the
French Revolution, the American Revolution, our own
Civil War, and the resistance to Adolph Hitler.

It would be naive and foolhardy to believe that we
are steadily and inevitably moving toward perfection,
for in America the top 5 percent of the people still earn
40 percent of the money and the bottom 20 percent earn

only 5 percent. This is the 1989 picture, worse than it looked in 1979, and 1979 was worse than 1969. No, we are not entering the kingdom yet. But the pressure will build on that income disparity, and if it gets worse, the pressure will increase. God has a stake in this. Human nature is not a self-directed evolutionary event without God's awareness. We are divinely created.

The earth is the LORD's, and the fulness thereof; the world, and they that dwell therein (Psalm 24:1).

The Ku Klux Klan was founded in Pulaski, Tennessee, in 1875. In 1989 the Klan decided to hold a parade celebrating the one hundred fourteenth year of its founding. It had begun in this isolated cotton town on Highway 64, a main artery through sharecropping central Tennessee, halfway between Memphis and Chattanooga. Progress has been slow in Pulaski, and I suppose the Klan felt that they could still count on intractable white hatred towards blacks and Jews, with blacks being intimidated by the white sheets, flaming torches, and large crosses. But by 1989 the white community had changed, and the blacks had changed and were no longer afraid. They had gained a new self-concept, a new dignity, and a new courage, and were far less likely to run from racist bigots. So when the parade came through town, the white people emptied the streets, closed up their shops, and let the Klan parade unnoticed. The evil that the Klan stood for had lost its following, and the victims were no longer available to them. Human nature has the potential to cope with the "demons" and to overcome. The long sweep of history testifies that human nature has consistently shown a propensity to contend with this carnal, atavistic inclination and to be released to spend its rich capacity for good.

If you could stand at Gibraltar in the year 1000 and look back toward the ancient world for the thousand years prior and then turn and look at the thousand years that followed, what you would see would be two vastly different worlds. And no one in his or her right mind

would trade the thousand years of the recent past for
the thousand years following the days of Jesus and the
apostle Paul. We have been confronted with our carnal,
earthy urges and drives that cause this idolatry, this materialism, the racism, and the xenophobia that have harassed us for all of these past thousand years. At the
same time, however, we are confronted with a divine
summons to something better, mindful of what those
first thousand years were like: humans fed to the lions
in the Roman circus, feudal serfs locked into an oppressed class permanently, churches controlled by
dukes and barons, women used only for childbearing
and drudgery on the farm and in the kitchen, education
for the elite only, laborers without voice about their condition of hire, the divine right of drunken, adulterous
kings . . . you name it.

We are not where we want to be, nor where we're going to be, but thank God, we're not where we were! The
wearisome persistence of the power of evil in history in-
clines us to become numb, callous, and unaware of the
actual shifts and changes that do occur and that give
witness to the good that stays in tension with the evil.

During the late 1950s when the South was envel-
oped in flaming rhetoric over school integration and
heated confrontations were frequent, Chaplain Wilker-
son invited me to preach in the Duke University chapel.
It was an honor for me, but a risk at the time for him. I
went and expected the best reception. Things went well,
but in the pulpit he whispered to me that I was the first
"colored"—that was the term of respect at that time—to
preach there. I could not believe that, knowing so many
renowned black ministers who normally might have
been invited to the Duke chapel. He explained that a previous president had committed himself not ever to have
a colored preacher there except over his dead body. He
had died, of course, and was buried in a crypt that was
located exactly beneath my feet as I stood preaching, a
colored preacher literally over his dead body!

In the 1830s Alexis de Toqueville toured America
and wrote his monumental description entitled *Democ-*

racy in America. He prophesied that among the future developments that he foresaw was a large-scale revolt of the blacks in the United States. Stranger that he was, nevertheless he recognized, a full generation before the Emancipation Proclamation, that the evil of slavery and the immorality of dehumanizing an entire people could not last.

When we stand back and take into view a comprehensive procession of the passing years, the evidence shows that this raw, carnal, survival equipment directly confronts the values that are generated in the human spirit, a gift from God that complements our fleshliness and out of which comes the capacity for moral excellence. As we look at this sweep of history, our faith grows that human nature can be harnessed, channeled, redeemed, and renewed.

After considering the possibility of the renewal of human nature on rather empirical and pragmatic grounds, we now turn to the Bible, to that body of experience that results from dealing with this issue most seriously for a long part of recorded human history. The Bible is a book of varied concerns, interests, and insights, but one topic that claims much of its attention is sin — the evil that is so much with us, the problem of human nature unharnessed, unrenewed, unchanneled, carnal, and earthy. The Bible is that slice of human history that focuses on God's relationship with humankind — spiritual history.

Many ways of understanding and writing history exist. One kind of history revolves around the exploration of continents by the explorers and seafarers; another history is based on wars and conquests — the Spartans versus the Athenians, the Medes versus the Persians, the Romans and the Goths, and the endless blood bath of the Crusades from Cornwall's craggy coast to the Arabian desert sands. Still another history traces medical advances from screaming blood-letting victims and dentists with hammers and chisels to laser eye surgery. Then there is the history of architecture from the pyramids to Saint Patrick's Cathedral. Yet another is the history of sports from the ancient Olympics to the Super Bowl. Finally, there is that history that the Bible, and only the Bible, deals with, and that is holy history—the story of sin and redemption—from the first man and woman naked in Eden to that multitude no one could number whom John saw standing before the Lamb in white robes. It is salvation's story, a very special kind of history. It is the record of how we have wrestled with the forces that have bound us to our carnal, earthy nature, our fleshliness and instincts that contend with us even now when we seek to impose on life a value system, a moral commitment, and the experience of a spiritual rebirth in Christ Jesus.

How shall they hear? The listeners need the most convincing evidence that we are created with possibilities for moral and spiritual renewal and maturity and that our creaturehood includes more than behavior based on survival instincts. We are all destined to live above the *indicative* mood, merely doing what comes next, as well as above the *imperative* mood, obeying commands and taking orders. We are moral beings with freedom and purpose, and we live in the *subjunctive* mood, with a sense of freedom and probability. We *may* and we *may not!* We reflect on our choices, consult our values, listen to the voice from within, and then engage our freedom and act. We have a sense of "perhaps" about us, and we are conscious of our options.

This Bible does not specialize in ancient geography; it is not a book on diets and cooking, not a book on medicine and healing, not a book on business, building construction, or farming, although much of it deals with these topics. The Bible is all about our alienation from God and our recovery, about our falling from innocence and our return, about our blundering and stumbling through life and the mercy of God that continues to lift and sustain us. When we look for a witness on the subject of human nature and its possibilities, no matter wherever else we may turn to find that hidden, persistent propensity towards goodness, to find the total fulfillment of our finest human capacities, and to see the flow of history toward something better, our task is incomplete until we turn to the book that has kept notes on this subject since Abraham came out of Ur of the Chaldees.

The Bible tells of the hatred that possessed the brothers of Joseph and of their selling him into slavery for twenty pieces of silver—human nature at its worst. But before the story ends, Joseph was in power in Egypt, and his brothers had to come to him for food to save their people from famine. Joseph had every opportunity to slay them, to enslave them, or to drive them away and let them starve, but we see the other side of human nature shining through. He ordered dinner to be prepared for them, had their feet washed, fed their donkeys, and set the table before them. After weeping over the sight of his baby brother Benjamin, Joseph asked for privacy to cry alone. He cried aloud and the whole palace staff wondered about him. After indulging himself in those tears, that mix of joy and pain, he called his brothers near and said, "I am Joseph, your brother whom ye sold into Egypt."

How shall they hear? They need to hear about Joseph and how he rejected the temptation to take sweet revenge and instead showed the possibilities for good in human nature.

The Bible presents to us young Queen Esther, comfortably situated as the king's favorite of all his harem, living in the luxury of exquisite oriental opulence and royal splendor. All of this she came into without anyone knowing that she was one of the rejected and persecuted people called Jews. When her people were about to be slain for not worshiping the king, she had a choice to make: She could conceal her identity and play it safe or go to the king and plead for the safety of her people. She knew the risks. The negative side of human nature asked her to try to save her position of privilege. The positive side of human nature called her to go to the king on behalf of her people saying, "If I perish, I perish."

The Bible shows Daniel in the king's court with power and authority and an easy life if he would deny his God. He used his authority to have his friends Shadrach, Meshach, and Abednego elevated to deputies over all the affairs of Babylon. When King Nebuchadnezzar made a gold statue of himself and called all of the captains, judges, sheriffs, and deputies together to fall down and worship or be thrown into the furnace, someone noticed that when the cornet, the flute, the harp, the sackbut, the psaltery, and the dulcimer all sounded and the worship of the king's image had begun, Shadrach, Meshach, and Abednego were standing up straight. Someone said, "O King, they serve not thy god, nor worship the golden image." The next king, Belshazzar, discovered that Daniel defied his decree to worship the king and deny his God. He found that in the face of the decree, Daniel opened his window wide toward Jerusalem three times a day and prayed where everyone could see him. The three Hebrew boys were thrown in the furnace and Daniel in the den of lions. The Bible celebrates the continuous victory of one child of God after another, a victory over mere survival and instinctive behavior.

Perhaps the most dramatic portrayal of the resilience and capacity of the human spirit can be found in the biography of Saul of Tarsus in the Acts of the Apostles. We find him at first as a fierce foe of Christ and the church, present at the stoning of Stephen and commissioned to track down and persecute Christians in Damascus. After his conversion and acceptance into the fellowship, he was constrained to use the same zeal and fervor in behalf of the faith that he had used against it. While he began by seeking to take the lives of others for believing in Jesus, he ended up declaring:

I am crucified with Christ; nevertheless I live; yet not I, but Christ liveth in me: and the life which I now live in the flesh I live by the faith of the Son of God, who loved me and gave himself for me (Galatians 2:20).

How shall they hear? What should they be listening for? People need to hear that the evidence that human nature can be redeemed abounds and that although we began as dust, "as many as received him, to them gave he power to become the sons of God" (John 1:12). Some of the press toward goodness is a trial-and-error development; some is from simple mutual and social experience and the slow process of acculturation; some is the fallout, here and there, of proximity to some of the special interventions of God, as the hand of the Eternal reached into time to call a Moses, a Joshua, an Elijah, an Isaiah, a Jeremiah, an Ezekiel, a John the Baptist, or to whisper to Mary the secret of the incarnation and the Word becoming flesh. But this raw nature of ours, this Adamic trace that enters the world with every new infant, is dealt with most particularly in the holy history of the Bible when the Son of God, who was without sin, became for all of us the Lamb slain on the altar to pay the ultimate price that we might know the transforming, renewing, restoring, integrative, sin-forgiving, guilt-removing, mind-changing, soul-warming, heart-healing, spirit-filling, power-availing, heaven-binding love of God.

This is more than a theological transaction. It is a homecoming for the soul, a rest for the weary, a victory for the battle worn, a shelter for every storm-tossed pilgrim, a kind of sweet relief.

> Jesus, Lover of my soul,
> Let me to Thy bosom fly,
> While the nearer waters roll,
> While the tempest still is high;
> Hide me, O my Savior, hide,
> Till the storm of life is past;
> Safe into the haven guide;
> O receive my soul at last![3]

---

[3]"Jesus, Lover of My Soul," by Charles Wesley.

FOUR

The Affirmation of Hope for a Genuine Human Community

We have become so accustomed to our narrow divisions, our polarization, and our insularity, our definition by social and economic class, race, religion, rank, and customs, that the preacher often finds herself or himself in a small and shrinking minority still believing in the hope for a genuine community in America and in the world.

In our time we have grown callous to the separations that we have learned to live with every day. We are wearied and worn down by the various tribalisms that constantly frustrate and inhibit movement toward a wider and more inclusive community and that remind us we are really *e pluribus non unum.*

Our biblical heritage, however, is replete with images of new and other kinds of relationships, such as the ones we find in the prophecy of Isaiah:

> The wolf shall dwell with the lamb,
> and the leopard shall lie down with the kid,

> and the calf and the young lion and the fat-
>   ling together,
> and a little child shall lead them . . .
> for the earth shall be full of the knowledge of
>   the LORD
> as the waters cover the sea.
>   — Isaiah 11:6, 9b, RSV

We have been obsessed with the notion that the human family can indeed become God's blessed community ever since John on Patmos heard the seventh angel blow his trumpet, with loud voices crying out, "The kingdom of the world has become the kingdom of our Lord and of his Christ, and he shall reign for ever and ever" (Revelation 11:15b, RSV).

From the fifth century B.C. we have inherited the beautiful story of Ruth, written in response to a period of heightened nationalism and isolation such as we find in the books of Ezra and Nehemiah. In the seminary we were taught that the fifth century B.C. witnessed a surge of nationalistic religious thinking, conceiving of God in very narrow terms. But by the end of the century we have the books of Ruth and Jonah responding to that narrowness. In Jonah the prophet was commissioned to preach to the former enemies of Israel, the Ninevites. In Ruth we have the story of a famine-struck family from Israel migrating into the territory of the Moabites, looking for food. They stayed a while, long enough for the two sons to marry Moabite women, Orpah and Ruth. The Moabites were descendants of Jews who had mixed with Babylonians, and the Israelites did not accept them.

As the story unfolds, the Israelite father and his two sons died, and Naomi, the Israelite mother-in-law, was left with two Moabite daughters-in-law. The time came when Naomi decided to return home and advised her daughters-in-law to remain among their own people. Orpah took her advice, but Naomi could not persuade Ruth to remain.

After Ruth and Naomi returned and settled in

Israel, a wealthy, respectable Israelite named Boaz married Ruth, the rejected alien from a mixed background. From their union David, Israel's greatest king, descended. What a message for Israel, that David descended from a Moabite! The Book of Ruth testifies to the capacity of the human spirit to transcend race and culture and to respond to the silent summons from within to relate to others in deep, warm, and enduring ways. This story is also a testimony to the strength and the self-determination of women in a world dominated by masculine heroes and male symbols of the strongest human virtues. In this ancient setting this story is a departure, and males are not the heroes. They all were weak and perished, and the stronger women worked things out.

When all the men had died of dreadful diseases and had vanished from view, these women were at center stage, and they celebrated the essence of community. Listen to Ruth's appeal to the heart of Naomi: " 'Entreat me not to leave you or to return from following you; for where you go I will go . . .' " (Ruth 1:16, RSV).

When the small band of followers of Jesus gathered in that upper room in Jerusalem to testify to his resurrection and to their experience of his presence in their midst, they felt the Holy Spirit descend in power. As they preached the Good News in the streets, persons of every race and clan gathered in a kaleidoscopic array praising God. The Holy Spirit had transcended their differences, and the record says that they were of one accord.

As Paul preached in Asia Minor and in the Mediterranean and Aegean cities and towns, the gospel confronted the crossroads of the world, the trade routes of long, slow, dusty camel caravans and the bustling merchant-shipping centers of that day. Roman officials, Jewish leaders, pagan magicians and sorcerers, women merchants, household slaves, Greek orators and poets, and priests of Artemis were all a part of his congregations. As this broad and inclusive representation of the human family became drawn into fellowship by the magnetism and the preaching of the gospel, little wonder that Paul could write:

> For ye are all the children of God by faith in Christ Jesus. For as many of you as have been baptized into Christ have put on Christ. There is neither Jew nor Greek, there is neither bond nor free, there is neither male nor female, for ye are all one in Christ Jesus (Galatians 3:26-28).

And yet, despite this summons to seek and find a basis for community in our strong and sacred tradition, the reality is still elusive. Each new generation seems to invent new reasons to defy movement toward a genuine human community. Many of the barriers to community remain with us from conflicts and unresolved tensions whose beginnings are buried in the hoary past. The Jewish-Palestinian strife can be traced back to the conquering of Palestine by the Seleucids in the second century B.C. The conflict between Protestants and Catholics in Northern Ireland began many generations ago. South Africa's shameful racial exploitation and inhuman subjugation dates back to the arrival of the Afrikaners in the seventeenth century. The United States is still slowly and tediously coming to terms with issues that have antecedents in the 244 years of chattel slavery in America. The tensions in our cities are due largely to inequalities and injustices that blacks will not tolerate and for which the proposed solutions are deemed intolerable by many of the white community.

Other barriers to community lie within us, in our own nagging fears and our fragile insecurity, in our idolatrous loyalty to the trappings of status, in our comfort and satisfaction with our ephemeral and transitory standing in the world of things, in our lazy and uncritical acceptance of half-truths and falsehoods about persons who differ from us, and in our enjoyment of arrogant notions about our self-assured superiority. All of these lead to a denial of genuine community.

Community is a mutual relationship between persons and groups based upon interests and values held in common. There are *national* communities, based upon cultural heritages such as those of the Japanese, Burmese, Indians, or Chinese that are shared among each national unit but barely beyond its own boundaries. There are *international* communities based upon common political, cultural, economic, or military interests such as the Warsaw Pact nations and the North Atlantic Treaty Organization. There are *supranational* communities—the Scandinavian states, the Arab states, the sub-Saharan African nations—who share common interests that reach within several contiguous national boundaries. Then there are *supernational* communities that exist above and without regard to national boundaries or for which such boundaries are really secondary: Roman Catholics, tennis players, Methodists, drug merchants, horse breeders, communists, genetic scientists, Free Masons, ballet dancers, Muslims, Pentecostals, Buddhists, nuclear physicists, the Baha'is, and a long list of associations and affiliations that transcend political, linguistic, racial, national, and cultural groupings. The ways in which we are capable of being bound together are infinite. Such smaller communities and networks are known best only by the long-distance telephone operators!

The hope and the possibility of genuine community rest firmly upon the basic understanding that all persons are indeed created equal. God did make of one blood all persons to dwell on the face of the earth. The circumstances of birth, the environment, the topography, the proximity to the equator, the North Pole, the mountains, the seas, the forests or the desert, and the historical details of the world that surround our coming clearly influence the way we look and dress, what we eat, how much comfort we learn to expect, and how much discomfort we learn to endure. Eskimos do not play baseball and Tahitians do not ski. The Jews of the Diaspora did not roam into the tropics or hike into Siberia. They went to more bearable climates on the rim of the Mediterranean.

Therefore, when Paul, Barnabas, Silas, Timothy, Titus, and John Mark set out to take the gospel of Jesus

Christ to the Jewish synagogues of Asia Minor and Europe, they planted churches everywhere they went — places where the weather was balmy and temperate and where it was conducive to writing books, playing violins and harps, building cathedrals, libraries, and universities. With the ideas of the Hellenic world, the Pax Romana, the availability of North African geometry and mathematics, and the concepts of the Judeo-Christian religions, and without desert winds, monsoon rains, and earthquakes, it was no surprise that the Mediterranean propinquity was a formidable advantage. No wonder that with such an advantage, nations so fortunate felt superior and promoted colonialism and slavery.

It has taken three hundred years for them to recognize that "the earth is the LORD's and the fullness thereof," and that God has made of one blood everybody. The idea of community carries us back to this fundamental truth and is the foundation for making deductions from that salient point.

Any inequalities among us have causes rooted somewhere. We must seek to find these causes that generate such disparities and deal with them. The outcomes of the disparities — the hunger, the thirst, the poverty, the disease, the ignorance, and the isolation — must be dealt with immediately from the benefits that we who live in more fortunate conditions take for granted.

Starting there, we build institutions of government, of philanthropy, of education and health care, and of religious and moral persuasion that seek to order our relations, to improve conditions that are adverse, and to stir up some excitement and enthusiasm about the good life.

This is why the preacher cannot keep still on this issue. Community will not happen on its own. It calls for sponsorship, promotion, urging, prompting, and celebration. How beautiful upon the mountain are the feet of those who preach!

When we become silent on community we are in complicity with *noncommunity*. The destruction in Iraq and the loss of so many lives is the consequence of a long and callous relationship of Western nations with the

Arab community. We used their oil and left them in the
Middle Ages in practically all other ways. We made
jokes about their cultural differences and isolated them.
One of the crying needs of the remaining decade of the
twentieth century is to undo the antipathies between the
Moslem and the Christian world and between the Moslem and the Jewish world and to find political solutions
that can accommodate the needs of each. When we see
community rejected, it comes about as a denial of our
common origin and our equal claims on life, liberty, and
the pursuit of happiness.

Many years ago I had the privilege of traveling
through the Near East — Turkey, Lebanon, Israel, Syria,
India, and Burma. It was a tour of American Baptist foreign mission institutions and a study of the transfer of
their colleges, churches, Bible schools, and health centers to the indigenous people. For nearly three months
my partners and I were simply intrigued by this micro-
cosmic view of the family of humankind — Buddhist,
Hindu, Islamic, Christian, and Jewish; rich and poor,
educated and illiterate; those aware of distances,
oceans, and continents, and those whose world was the
size of Delaware. Our minds and souls were stretched.
Before we could get used to the thin, small features, the
silken hair, the mahogany complexion, and the deadly
serious staccato accent of the people of India, we were
in Burma among full, round faces, heavy, coarse,
straight hair, stocky frames, and musical language.
Then we shuttled back to the Arab world where there
were chiseled features, swarthy complexions, good hu-
mor, and almost childish simplicity.

Our study group included a person of Scandinavian
ancestry with blond hair and light eyes, a Philadelphian
with a Scotch-Irish background, and a Virginian of slave
descent. Eating, laughing, praying, sleeping, debating,
and singing together, we confronted the variety of
peoples we met as one. It was an experience of community with all of its breadth, depth, and diversity.

When I returned to the States, I had to make a report to the American Baptist Foreign Mission Society in

session at Green Lake, Wisconsin. Since I had been away so long, my wife and I decided to make a little vacation of the trip from Virginia Union University in Richmond to Green Lake, Wisconsin. It was fun to watch her face register every human emotion as I gave her a two-day, nonstop audio record of all I had seen and heard. We laughed at the funny and embarrassing incidents and spoke quietly and empathetically about the poverty and disease that I had witnessed.

After clearing Chicago's rush-hour traffic (this being before the superhighways were built), we eased into wide-open Wisconsin. Hunger and fatigue beckoned us to stop at a handsome restaurant and to enjoy some honest, midwestern cooking. After we were seated, we waited for a full half-hour for a waiter. Finally, the same lady who had seated us came back and told us in tears that she had been instructed to invite us to leave because "we were not members of their club." It was no club. It was racial rejection and noncommunity.

Imagine how the Green Lake audience felt when, after giving them a report of my rare, mind-stretching experience across three continents and sharing my positive feelings about the Baptist contributions to the total human family, I had to add the fact that at home, the "land of the free and the home of the brave," my wife and I were run out of a clean, well-appointed restaurant north of Chicago in the great state of Wisconsin. Noncommunity.

While teaching at Rutgers, I had much fun visiting high schools in New Jersey and Long Island, introducing white students and teachers to black history and the need for greater understanding. On most visits the results were positive and assuring. On a visit to a school in an upper-middle-class New Jersey town, suburban to Philadelphia, there was a Martin Luther King, Jr., commemoration with the most articulate, scholarly, well-groomed black students in charge. They were so impressive that their sponsor, a black guidance counselor, beamed with pride.

Then they found out that some white schoolmates

had hidden a portrait of Dr. King that they had planned to display, and when I stood at the lectern to speak, the entire first row raised newspapers to their faces and hid themselves from my view. We were crushed that this could happen in such an enlightened and prosperous community where the adult black population was mostly professional and the black children were making honor grades.

Thank God, however, that the response to the call to community is frequently different. At the University of New Hampshire a kindergarten teacher approached me after a lecture and begged me to add a visit to her class to my grueling schedule. I did, and the result was that one little one came and put his white hand on my brown hand and said, "Brown is pretty!" No one had gotten to them to corrupt their minds with the message of non-community. Instead, their teacher was trying to immunize them against such hatred.

As remote and far-fetched as the idea of community may seem, those who preach cannot escape the imperative to make clear God's prevailing and enduring love for the whole human family. They must create a restlessness and a dissatisfaction with the divisiveness of God's family, the hardened attitudes that permit hatred to thrive. The listeners must feel indignant about the enormous suffering that so many must endure as a concomitant to our blindness toward one another's needs and our lack of empathy toward those who suffer. Like Tennyson in "Locksley Hall," we, too, need a vision, a new paradigm, a compelling imperative to affirm the possibility of community:

> For I dipped into the future, far as human eye could
> see,
> Saw the Vision of the world, and all the wonder that
> would be;
>   . . .
> Till the war drum throbbed no longer, and the battle
> flags were furled
> In the parliament of man, the federation of the world.

There the common sense of most shall hold a fretful
    realm in awe
And the kindly earth shall slumber, lapped in univer-
    sal law.

While such a community may find support in secular quarters, the Christian preacher, however, should
find this to be one of the most important arrows in his or
her quiver, one of the most crucial messages to bear to
the people. We believe that God came in Christ to save
the *whole* world, to redeem the *entire* human race, and
to affirm the hope that the human family can indeed
achieve a genuine community. The preacher has the
privilege and the opportunity of lifting up those themes
in the gospel of Christ that provide a basis for such a
genuine community.

The kingdom of God that Jesus and John the Baptist
preached did indeed reach across all of the distinctions
of race and culture. When the followers of John complained that they were already sons of Abraham and did
not need to join the new kingdom of God, John told them
that God could make sons of Abraham out of stones. The
kingdom was a new allegiance with no reference to a
bloodline or an ethnic origin. And the kingdom never
seems so much like a structured, geographic organization or program as it is a controlling, constraining force
in the hearts of persons under the rule of God's love.
Such persons function in kingdom ways where they are,
and as they do, the kingdom spreads and the rule of
God's love expands among the persons of the world.

Such a level of community allows for that richness,
diversity, and authenticity of life that comes while being
loyal to one's own traditions and folkways. But it calls us
to add to such important ethnic identities a larger identity with values capable of dealing with the more profound aspects of the common life of all humankind on
planet Earth.

When I joined the board of directors of the Christian Children's Fund several years ago, I was shocked to
discover that there on that quiet corner of Third and

Cary Streets in Richmond, Virginia, in the headquarters of this international service organization, was a beehive of activity raising $90 million a year to educate, clothe, and provide health care for 500,000 of the world's poorest children. Across these years, some of the most fruitful hours I have spent have been in committee meetings and board deliberations on what and how to do for these half a million children. We offer the public a chance to join in by providing a mere twenty-one dollars a month (the cost, perhaps, of one dinner out for one person) to meet the needs of one of these children for a *month*.

One of our young friends whom my wife and I support lives in Gambia—a Moslem student attending a Catholic school, speaking a local dialect and Arabic. Our other friend is a junior high school girl from a large, poor family in Uganda. We are black Baptists from Virginia, speaking "tidewater English"! We have never seen either of them; they send pictures and letters. What is important is that something calls us to reach out to them—across the three thousand miles that separate us, across distinctions of religion, language, and culture—and to share our means with them, to save them from hunger, disease, and illiteracy. We hold on to our identity as black Baptists from Virginia, but we take on a larger identity when we participate as persons concerned with human needs everywhere, even supporting a schoolboy in Gambia and a schoolgirl in Uganda.

It is refreshing to experience the voluntary and spontaneous response of persons who differ so much, even if it is brief and very specific. In the summer of 1989, my wife and I attended a "get down" Ray Charles jazz concert on Cape Cod. In college I earned my room and board playing the alto saxophone with the Virginia State Trojan Jazz Band, and I still enjoy the artistry of jazz musicians and their improvisations. It helps me to step back for a moment from life's heavy engagements for a breather. We were on Cape Cod in the Melody Tent at Hyannis. The place was filled with people of every description—vacationers from Boston and New York City, local senior retirees, wealthy "old money" resi-

dents, young honeymooners, and students employed for
the summer. The majority of the audience was white,
and Ray Charles is black, born blind, poor, and or-
phaned. His band is one-half black; his five female sing-
ers are black. His singing is *very* black, bluesy, throaty,
sensuous, original, and deeply soul.

What on earth caused all of these white people on
Cape Cod to spend twenty-six dollars each to sit for
three hours through boring amateur preliminaries to
hear forty-five minutes of guttural blues from a blind,
black balladeer? Well, deep down inside there is something primordial about us that cries for expression. It is
in us all—Texans, Russians, Koreans, Australians, and
Cape Codders. Ray Charles is only one of many who
have found it, and he celebrates it. He almost falls off
the piano stool celebrating it! This diverse crowd
screamed and yelled with pure and uninhibited delight.
In fact, a young black woman journalist from the Soviet
Union visiting the United States on an exchange program informed us that all over Moscow young people listened avidly to the sounds of Michael Jackson and
Stevie Wonder. Even the Iron Curtain was penetrated by
such subtle, irresistible expressions of human common-
ality. The potential for oneness is there! It is found at
this subrational, subliminal level, and it is surely found
at other levels too.

Preachers are obliged to point to obvious symbols
of noncommunity in order to focus on the hope, the
need, the possibility of change. When we consider the
human condition in the time of Jesus, we are amazed at
the way he dealt with the persons he encountered.
Lepers were feared, ostracized, and avoided; blind persons were regarded as bearing the punishment for their
own sins or someone else's; harlots and publicans were
beyond the bounds of the religious community; but Jesus was a friend to them all. Jesus saw persons not in
the light of their failures, but in the light of their personhood and their significance as God's children. Despite the exigent circumstances of their lives, as
creatures of God they were significant.

Nothing is clearer in the Gospels than the story of the rich man and Lazarus, the beggar at his gate. The portrait of the rich man is thorough. He dined sumptuously every day, while Lazarus, with dogs licking his sores, waited for the crumbs from the rich man's table. Jesus clearly meant for us to see the extremes represented in this situation. But the circumstances changed, and each came before God only in his essential personhood. The gate, the dining table, the dogs were all missing. In the final judgment both the rich man and Lazarus were on the same plane, except that the beggar had made it to heaven and the rich man had missed it by far.

When we preach about the possibility of community, it is important for us to save our people from the illusion that the distinctions created by poverty and by historic exclusion and isolation mean more than they do. Beneath such distinctions persons *are* equal. When we acknowledge this equality, we authenticate other persons who have been so victimized.

On the tidy, graceful campus of Presbyterian College in Clinton, South Carolina, there is a handsome colonial brick building named Martha Dendy Hall. Two generations earlier, when there were only a couple of hundred students there, a black laundress could be seen two or three times a day crossing the campus in the shadows of towering oak and elm trees, silent witnesses to years of slavery. She walked alone in quiet contemplation, with a large straw basket skillfully balanced on her head crowning her clean, dark face ridged firmly and deeply with resolution and determination. I heard that she not only laundered the students' clothes but also counseled them on matters of dress, drinking, personal salvation, sex, politeness, and respect for others. She was a campus conscience. When the young white men whose clothes she once laundered became trustees, they remembered her. Consequently, in the atmosphere of South Carolina politics in the sixties, when there were heated debates on school integration, these white college trustees named this handsome new building in the sacred memory of their black laundry lady.

All of Harlem rejoiced when they heard that Princess Diana of England, while visiting New York City in the spring of 1989, insisted that Harlem Hospital and the children's AIDS ward be placed on her itinerary. We had known of her planned visits to the elegant jewelry stores, to the art galleries, and to the exclusive teas and soirées, but we were shocked that she wanted to visit Harlem to see the children born to AIDS victims who were infected and destined to die early. She picked up a little boy on that ward, held him in her arms and whispered to him. No one learned what she said. How ironic—one representing so-called royal blood and enormous wealth and prestige went out of her way to signify to the world the real status in God's sight of a child with AIDS.

Our world is cynical, and in order to maintain hope for community, the preacher must be alert to every sign of emerging community that can be found. It will not be through calm, cold, calculating logic that we will maintain this hope. Someone will have to be persuasive and insistent that we are all God's children, that we are equal, and that our interests are mutual.

Economic, educational, and political differences have stratified us so as to make equality seem remote, but as the gospel is preached, the reality of God comes a bit closer. We don't look for God's kingdom in our own institutions, monuments, shrines, roads, tunnels, and skyscrapers. Instead, we see our witness here more as a gift, a blessing, and a benefit. In this light, we see God as everyone's Creator and the earth as God's handiwork. Our equality is then much better understood and appreciated.

"O LORD, our Lord, how excellent is thy name in all the earth! who hast set thy glory above the heavens.

. . .

When I consider thy heavens, the work of thy fingers, the moon and the stars, which thou hast ordained; What is man, that thou art mindful of him? and the son of man, that thou visitest him? For thou hast made him a little lower than the angels, and hast crowned him with glory and honour (Psalm 8:1,3–5).

After we accept the Christian understanding of equality of all persons before God as the first basis for hope in a genuine community, then we accept *agape*, selfless love. The love that Jesus taught says a great deal about the one who is loved and the nature of our interest in other persons. Selfless love is not simple-minded naiveté, but an acting out of our interest in others, our response to others where they are, how they are, and *why* they are as they are! This flows from our view of them as objects of God's love, as we are also. This unmeasured love flows from our awareness of God's love for all of us. True love is always the willingness to take the initiative in seeking good in the life of another. *Agape* is the kind of love that expects nothing in return and does not require of the recipient any special qualification.

Many persons inhibit our love for them because they do seem unworthy; selfless love, therefore, must depend upon something more compelling than the *appeal* of the person to be loved. This does not work at all unless it is the outpouring of good will that comes from a heart touched by the love of God. Because we have seen so little of this in a crass, materialistic, power-hungry, money-loving, secular culture, we do find it hard to embrace a notion of genuine community.

I have a habit of asking taxi drivers in Washington, D.C., if they ever had a Peace Corps teacher. It seems that all D.C. cabs are driven by students from Africa! Almost without exception a driver will turn quickly to me and start describing a Peace Corps teacher. This is done with the most spontaneous smile of good will, because the Peace Corps volunteer teacher, as a rule, made herself or himself a part of the life of the community without making silly comparisons. The volunteer entered into the lives of the people as, how, and where they were. One could observe on the slightest contact how gently and easily these giving young people — and some not so young — bridged the chasm of language, culture, reli-

gion, and economic difference. It was *agape* love at
work, and because it is such selflessness, it generates a
response of similar selflessness. This is the kind of love
that Jesus introduced into the whole human equation. It
is truly something to preach about in keeping hope alive
for a genuine community.

Anyone who sees this as impractical should examine the consequences of rejecting such love, closing all
channels for expressing such love, leaving races, nations, and the various cultures of the world waiting for
each new relationship to be a begrudging, bartered exchange, a *quid pro quo*, like foreign policies that keep
wars going on somewhere all the time!

During the days of harsh racial separation and inequality, one of the secrets about life in the South that
kept such a tenuous and volatile situation from explod-
ing was that on those farms, in those kitchens, on those
mule-drawn wagons, and in those sweltering barns
there were black *and* white persons working daily side
by side. They would often lose sight of the line that the
laws and customs required them to observe, the unfair
and arbitrary racial stratification, and would reach out
to one another with a love that was stronger than all of
the prohibitions and taboos that were there to thwart it.

My sainted grandmother, talking with us clearly
while in her nineties, explained that the Fisher family,
her slavemasters, allowed her to sit in the circle with the
white children when the Episcopal minister would
come by to tutor them on their Chesterfield County
plantation. And later, while the postbellum resentment
was still high and antiblack feelings fueled lynch mobs
and compelled racial separation laws, that same Fisher
family sent little Hattie Ann, my grandmother, to Hampton Institute and paid all of her expenses. All of this was
grossly incongruous with a slave system and the atmosphere of the Reconstruction in Chesterfield County, Virginia.

It is the most earnest level of trust in God when a
preacher shows enough faith to preach about the possibility of this kind of love in the face of a culture that

needs to be sold on it. And the preacher, therefore, cannot afford to be the *last* one to proclaim such selfless love. He or she must be the first! Jesus said: "Love your enemies, bless them that curse you, do good to them that hate you, and pray for them which despitefully use you . . ." (Matthew 5:44).

Perhaps the toughest test for us in extending love to the undeserving is to make such love institutional and a part of the political consensus. It is one thing to find an individual exemplar of selfless love here and there, a true saint, renowned or obscure; but a sustained and strategic effort is necessary to translate something so individual and esoteric as selfless love (with no specific gravity, no standard deviation, no molecular weight—none of these tangibles—but an attitude toward persons that we learned from Jesus), to give it applicability, and to fight for it in public programs and in legislation.

Helping to make selfless love a part of the society's agenda and institutionalizing it is the preacher's greatest challenge. It may require enlisting actively in local politics to correct a glaring evil or to monitor the uses of power; it may mean raising money for the legal defense of an unpopular person who is right; it may mean risking one's pulpit for telling the truth about a public neglect; it may mean walking a picket line or boycotting a merchant for insulting helpless people. This challenge could call for testifying before a legislative committee or joining parents in a school protest against an uncaring, indifferent, dysfunctional school administrator. Who knows? But selfless love cannot remain inactive, poetic sentiment mouthed in the stillness of the cathedral, a vain and insipid gesture toward goodness without serious intention.

The kinds of "for instances" that we find in the ministry of Jesus must be found in our ministry as well. Converting the Jericho Road into our own road and the good Samaritan into our own model is the preacher's task. Standing like the prodigal's father in the road waiting to start the party for every prodigal who returns home is worth preaching and hearing about.

Our people are bombarded by commercial advertising with reminders to be self-regarding, to be narcissistic, to be concerned about the style of our clothes, the smoothness of our skin, the speed of our cars, the expanding of our waistlines, and the receding of our hairlines. Our colleges and universities are jammed with waves of students majoring in advertising, merchandising, management, and marketing—learning to motivate all of us to want more and more and more.

The entire popular frame of reference is sensate, physical, greedy, idolatrous, and competitive for egoistic delights. The preacher has the obligation to remind us of the sin of such idolatry, to turn our faces toward the God of heaven so that we recognize we are not alone in the world, to call us to our higher destiny, to invite us to consider moderating love of self, and for God's sake, to learn to let selfless love flow from heart to heart and from breast to breast. This is the preacher's special assignment. No one else in society is assigned the task of tilting our lives Godward and correcting our perspective on life. Listen to the prophet of Israel:

> Ho, every one that thirsteth, come ye to the waters, and he that hath no money; come ye, buy, and eat; yea, come, buy wine and milk without money and without price. Wherefore do ye spend money for that which is not bread? and your labour for that which satisfieth not? hearken diligently unto me, and eat ye that which is good, and let your soul delight itself in fatness. Incline your ear, and come unto me; hear, and your soul shall live . . . (Isaiah 55:1–3a).

As we turn from the self-indulgent, pampering, corrosive self-love that leads to narrowness, racism, supernationalism and endless wars and begin to spread the good news of healing, self-ennobling, cleansing, joyful, and redemptive selfless love, as surely as night follows day and the darkness fades into the dawn, genuine community will begin to emerge.

We do indeed affirm the hope of community in the world as we preach the equality and selfless love that Jesus initiated. In the same message from the Gospels we find compassion, the capacity to share the suffering and the pain of another. This bears further witness to the hope of real community in the world.

On a trip to Norfolk State University recently, I met a young African college student visiting that community for a neurosurgical operation. He was a third-year student at the University of Liberia. He told me that he was from a village where there were 250 young men of his age group and only two had completed high school. The cost of leaving home and boarding at a high school miles away was simply out of reach for most families.

He was brought to Norfolk by a concerned and compassionate group called Operation Smiles, volunteers who raise thousands of dollars a year to send medical and social work teams abroad to find cases where unavailable surgery is needed and feasible. They then perform the surgery there or bring the more serious ones back to better-equipped facilities.

This young man from Liberia had had lockjaw, a form of tetanus that prevented him from chewing or speaking clearly. But when I saw him he could smile, chew, talk, laugh, and debate! The surgeons in Norfolk had opened the right side of his cranium, made the corrections, and set him free! His poverty had dictated that he would spend a lifetime mumbling between his firmly locked teeth and slurping liquids through a quill. But Operation Smile was made up of a handful of persons who acknowledged the equality of God's children and who practiced selfless love. All of that led them to suffer with a student with lockjaw three thousand miles away whom they had never seen and did not know. My soul! Let that be the paradigm of what genuine community would be if we followed that example, "the strong bearing the infirmities of the weak." This is the New Testament alive in the modern world. This is the mind of Christ in our midst.

Such conduct on our part will indeed penetrate barriers of race, class, nationhood, and culture, and connect us in wonderful ways. The persons who started Operation Smile are church-going people. Their lives have been touched by the fragrance of the gospel. They have sat still in Sunday morning sanctuaries where a sensitive, kingdom-dwelling, community-extending preacher was not afraid to "own His cause" and did not "blush to speak His name." While worshiping, they felt a new center for their lives taking shape. At first it felt strange and new, but after a while it felt like the only way to focus. Their imaginations began to dance to thought, ideas, plans, and programs that would give a new "for instance" to this new kingdom of thinking.

> Consecrate me now to Thy service, Lord,
> By the power of grace divine;
> Let my soul look up with a steadfast hope,
> And my will be lost in Thine.[1]

From the gospel the preacher should proclaim equality, selfless love, and compassion. And from the gospel of Christ the preacher should also proclaim justice and fairness. This is indeed another linchpin of genuine community. Much of the suffering of Jesus' day came from injustice and unfairness. Jesus was always on the case of those who had unfairly emerged as persons of means. He encouraged thrift, planning, and even investing for profit, but it is abundantly clear that he was suspicious of the rich of his day. Jesus did not congratulate the man building bigger barns and the rich ruler on their success!

Justice is often neglected in some circles in which earnest evangelical preaching thrives. In the 1960s I was sent to visit a world-renowned evangelist who ended up calling Jesus a "liberal." In three continents we have a history of three hundred years of Europeans colonizing persons, controlling their governments, and draining away their raw materials. The corollary to this was to sell them a religious outlook that made them docile and compliant, to leave them uneducated, and to create an appetite for things and a greedy lifestyle that promoted corruption.

---

[1] "I Am Thine, O Lord," by Fanny J. Crosby.

When colonialism ended, very few new nations had the trained personnel to take over the reins of government, industry, science, medicine, education, and technology. The overpopulation, the governmental corruption, the abuse of resources, and the slow pace of development have historical antecedents in the three hundred years of colonialism which ended less than fifty years ago. One of the most cruel consequences of that era is the pervasive and enduring racism that is *endemic* injustice.

The community that we hope for is frustrated by the awful disparities in opportunity and quality of life between the former colonies and the former colonizers. And it is not fair. Jesus gave the most succinct basis for fairness and justice when he said, "as ye would that men should do to you, do ye also to them likewise" (Luke 6:31).

John Rawls, in his book *A Theory of Justice*, challenges us to look again at those nineteenth-century assumptions about justice: the greatest good for the greatest number—John Stuart Mill; survival of the fittest, natural selection—Charles Darwin. "Nature," of course, had little to do with the invention of slavery and colonialism. The "selection" took place at the barrel of a gun! We are not where we are because of what *nature* required. The strong did not always become strong naturally, but more often by abusing other people by force. And also, the greatest good for the greatest number begs the question, Who decides what is the greatest good? Of course! The greatest number! Somewhere there ought to be a canon for fairness that we can all look to in search of justice.

Justice, when applied domestically and worldwide, may not accomplish all that it intends, but as it is promulgated and put into action, it may have a sustained and promising effect. If preachers lifted up the notions of equality, selfless love, and compassion, this idea of justice would be better understood, and the idea of genuine community would be better understood.

When the impetus for genuine community is lost

and the momentum has become undermined by passive inertia; when the celebrations of the human potential for true community have faded into a faint diminuendo; when the voices that should herald every sign of new movement toward a higher and nobler consensus are mumbling inarticulate, pious slogans and fumbling with the icons of a lingering and weary tribalism, the kind of vacuum is created that nature abhors. Then the most vicious, violent, and vile behavior moves in. It is so clear why Jesus said that those who were not *with* him were against him. In moral matters there is no neutral ground.

Los Angeles is the most completely diverse city in the world. Texas cowboys; Japanese merchants; Mexican laborers and students; African American recording artists, musicians, and politicians; Native Americans from the foothills of the Rocky Mountains; the children of German, Scandinavian, Italian, Irish, Eastern European, and British immigrants of three generations ago experimenting with life at the margins; robed priests of young religions soliciting new recruits from disenchanted Catholics, Jews, Methodists, and Baptists; and tinseled, plastic, voluble con artists of every stripe and hue who are committed to live without labor fill the streets, the stores, the airports, the restaurants, and the television screens. What a potent place to pilot the notion of genuine community! But the facts are different. The ethnic processions are cold, distant, and xenophobic and pass one another like ships in the night. So when one sees white policemen on television pounding on the head, shoulders, rib cage, and groin of a handcuffed African American crime suspect, taking turns swinging their forty-inch oak clubs with wild and savage abandon, it is only one more consequence of predictable noncommunity.

Likewise, Saddam Hussein with his aberrant behavior is the predictable outcome of the estrangement between East and West, Arab and Jew, Moslem and Christian, and the oil-producing and oil-consuming nations. Historic antipathies have lingered since the eleventh, twelfth, and thirteenth centuries when those nine military campaigns called the Crusades left a trail of blood from Gibraltar to the Syrian desert. The conversations and exchanges between these two worlds have been businesslike, guarded, untrusting, and limited — selling guns and buying oil without love, understanding, or compassion.

Mr. Hussein was left to believe that no one would really care if he took Kuwait. After all, no one cared about Kuwait's permanent, anachronistic, feudal plutocracy, just as no one paid any attention to South Africa's inhuman racial arrangement for centuries.

When we forsake the summons to recognize the dignity and worth of all of God's children, deny to others our charity and our skill in creating a higher quality of life for our total humanity, and reject the fundamentals of justice and fairness, we forsake genuine community. The result is the kind of noncommunity represented by the previously mentioned incident — a Los Angeles police gang in uniform (filmed by an unnoticed amateur photographer on March 4, 1991, and shown on television worldwide) violently beating an African American suspect with their night sticks.

When we allow the United Nations to become weakened by major powers, behaving unilaterally in their own interests all over the world, and then cripple voluntary international witnesses with small budgets, fragmentary staffing, and begrudging participation, we frustrate movement toward a world of understanding and peace. The alternative is to ship a militarized city of 500,000 fighting personnel 6,000 miles away from home, spending $60 billion killing Iraqi men, women, and children and causing great destruction. That same money could have gone for food and medicine for dying children all over the world, for homeless shelters in New York and Milwaukee, for scholarships for our latent geniuses and those late entrants into the world of advanced schooling, and for offsetting the health costs that are causing skyrocketing hospital deficits.

This scenario makes it imperative for God's

preachers to make the case for community on a regular basis, with choirs singing, organs pealing, and the strongest metaphors and analogies put to the service of this compelling cause. This arrow must fly from the preacher's quiver.

Every now and then we find an outstanding example of how a person sensitive to the claims of justice and fairness acts in an impressionable "for instance." If we could imagine such behavior magnified and amplified many times over in situations of all types and dimensions, it would become clear to us how fairness and justice, as Rawls presents them, become the ultimate basis for community.

I recently visited and gave a chapel talk at that same small campus in South Carolina where the student center was named after the laundry lady. After the service, the president, Dr. Orr, and I were walking slowly along a campus path. We were overtaken by a young man who thanked me for my presentation. He was big, hefty, and muscular, and beside him stood a young woman about three feet, five inches tall, smiling in agreement with him. In my shock at seeing this small person with this big, thick-framed fellow, I leaned down, patted her on the shoulder, and wished her good luck and God's blessings. But my gaze must have embarrassed her.

Then President Orr explained that they were not only brother and sister, but twins! I was not ready for that. What a genetic trick, one above average in height and the other of unusually short stature. As I listened further, I learned that he had been recruited by several football "powers," but he had made it clear that he would attend whatever college provided a scholarship for his sister. He was a "hot" recruit and could have gone to a college that would have given him television exposure and a good chance for a professional contract. But he rejected such exposure for himself in order to be certain that his sister would not be laughed at, ignored, treated like a circus exhibit, ostracized, or humiliated. He recognized that he had been born with benefits that he had not earned and that she had been born with an enor-

mous deficit that she had not earned or deserved. He
was willing to adjust his life's chances to share her
struggle, to divide his "social capital" with her, and enhance her chances for those outcomes that we all cher-
ish. Such is a paradigm of justice and fairness. When
enlarged to fit the inequality of opportunity that exists
everywhere, it becomes a basis for social renewal and
genuine community.

FIVE

Awareness of the Eternal in the Midst of Time

What we do in churches and temples is qualitatively different from all other gatherings of persons and all other rituals and ceremonies. It is different because of the frame of reference. We deal with the deep center of human existence and the extreme outer perimeter. We are concerned with things that are ultimate.

The toughest test that one can face in moral and spiritual growth is to find a way to live *in* the real world of practicality and compromise without becoming *of* that world. At the hour of worship, persons are listening for some help on the degree to which an ordinary person can become entangled with the process of attaining reasonable security and striving for personal success. How involved can one become in the total syndrome of material accomplishment—mastering the art of hedging one's future against economic disaster, embracing those trappings of prominence that success will confer, responding to the drive toward higher and higher achievement, monitoring the promotion of children into fruitful and fulfilling adulthood, building protection against abuse and abandonment in old age—and still remain a candidate for the kingdom of God that Jesus proclaimed?

Behind the sermon that Jesus preached on the Mount of Olives was his desire that we should all keep a safe distance from the concupiscent, alluring, ensnaring, and tentative enticements of this world and focus on becoming children of our heavenly Father, dwelling in the kingdom. All of the language of that sermon of Jesus in Matthew 5, 6, and 7 speaks to a kind of dual citizenship: one being a rapprochement with the visible, tangible, physical, spatial, temporal world, and the other a response to the spiritual world that is just as real—that everpresent, eternal order that is shot through our earthbound existence. It is in this tension, this area of negotiation, of compromise, of conciliation that we all must live, with more or less balance, poise, and integrity.

Jesus lays a heavy demand on us in Matthew 5, 6, and 7. He asks us to let our conduct be so exemplary that it will cause others to glorify God. He asks us not only to fulfill the minimal requirements of the Commandments, but also to go beyond their proscriptions with an even higher moral accountability. He asks us to put reconciliation with our neighbor above offering gifts at the altar; he asks us even further to love persons who hate us.

Jesus teaches us to be sincere rather than showy in our worship and to pray in very simple, plain words. He asks us to love things eternal more than money and personal security and not to count on the permanence of material things. He asks us not to be anxious and fretful about tomorrow because God will provide for us, just as God feeds the birds of the air and clothes the lilies of the field. He asks us not to measure, inspect, and grade the conduct of another's life, but to spend that time scrutinizing our own.

At the end of Matthew 5 he asks us to be perfect. And this keeps us busy for a lifetime trying to satisfy our daily, mundane, pressing demands, providing care for those for whom we are responsible, while trying at the same time to remain in tune with the Spirit of the living God.

The preacher who reaches for our attention on Sunday morning must know what this tension is like from his or her own experience and, therefore, should be aware of the vibrations, queries, moods, and needs of the waiting congregation. While this may be the most ill-defined task, the most nebulous assignment of all, the most exhausting function that a preacher must serve, no one else is set apart and commissioned to continue to remind persons that we are a very special creation, above the entire order of all created things and that we are uniquely destined for fellowship with God. The Gospel of Matthew says that Jesus taught with authority, with a kind of insider's knowledge. He came preaching the Good News that the kingdom of God was a constant, present-potential-eternity bending low into time; and despite our fragile fleshliness, we are called to repent, to believe, and to take up our kingdom membership while still struggling in the world of space and time. Eternity begins now. This is indeed good news and it becomes a very important arrow in the preacher's quiver.

I recall a conference of pastors at Green Lake, Wisconsin, many years ago. At one session we were all on a spacious, neatly trimmed lawn, sitting on the shores of a shining lake in the stillness of a crisp summer morning. The surface of those deep, shimmering, emerald waters reflected the warm glow of the morning sunlight, and nature enfolded all of us in the casual magic and innocent charm of that perfect day. We were awaiting the arrival of our lecturer for the week, Dr. Clarence Jordan, the leader of Koinonia, an experimental community in Georgia that defied our easy accommodations to materialism and racism. Dr. Jordan was an apostle of simplicity, humility, sincerity, and peace; he lived it with or without popular support and approval.

As we waited anxiously, wondering what we would do if he did not show up (and some, no doubt, wondering as well what we would do *if he did!*), we heard the putter-

ing of an old, two-cylinder motorcycle that sounded like
a lawn mower. We saw an approaching cyclist covered
with grimy road dust, disheveled in his riding gear, moving straight toward us. He had bunked down somewhere
overnight and made an early-morning appearance before he had time to clean up. He preferred not to delay us
any longer and hastened immediately to the front, with
his back to the lake. He searched us with his slow, pene-
trating gaze. The contrast between his mode of travel
and ours and between his total life's commitment and
that of most of us caused the guilt in our group to be
thick enough to slice with a knife.

He began. His very presence in wrinkled working
clothes, with no signs of American affluence attached to
him, made the well-dressed clergy audience feel embarrassed, unworthy, and unclean. He went through the sermon of Jesus in Matthew 5, 6, and 7 tediously from a
hand-size Greek New Testament. He paused and lingered at the passage on adultery and dwelled on the
whole matter of motives and intentions. He explained
that lusting was as much of a sin as actual adultery. He
paused again on the point of nonviolence and emphasized the need for redemptive suffering, for turning the
other cheek when smitten rather than resisting evil. All
of this, he explained, we would do in order (according to
Matthew 5:45) that we might be the children of our
Father *which is in heaven,* in order that we might taste
eternity now and here. As he neared the end of the sermon, he emphasized that we should take the initiative in
doing good for others.

Clearly, this message of Christ came from an understanding of spiritual reality above and beyond the mundane priorities of ordinary living. One minister stood up
and asked with temerity, "Dr. Jordan, realistically, how
can one be a successful, modern, urban pastor and follow the sermon of Jesus on the Mount of Olives?" Jordan
replied: "Jesus did not give this sermon to successful,
modern, urban pastors. He gave it to his *disciples,* and if
there is a conflict, you have to choose whether you are

going to be a disciple or a successful, modern, urban pastor." Jordan had heightened the tension.

We are in the world, but at the same time we should be aware of our real and abiding spiritual home. The term "kingdom of God" is a first-century metaphor. We do not have a king today, and the term "kingdom" is not common to our own experience. But everyone in Jesus' time knew what a "kingdom" was. It meant rulership, the reign of God in our lives. And even though the metaphor is dated, we know what Jesus meant. He meant that beyond this transient dream is the eternal God, from everlasting to everlasting, who does not change.

Every believer seated before the preacher on Sunday morning is ranked somewhere on a scale of one to ten on how well he or she has resolved this issue: How much response do I give to the *world* and to those practical claims made on me, and how will I allow such a response to deflect me from seeking the kingdom of God and God's righteousness?

We are troubled even more grievously when we realize how fully and completely some persons have been able to manage life with a minimal accommodation to material comfort and with a total involvement in acts of compassion and selfless love. What do they know, we ask, that has escaped us? Do they have some special equipment that we have missed? How can some persons wear the persistent demands of the carnal dimension of this life like a loose garment?

This raises a question about how ministers are trained in the first place. It is a mistake, I believe, for preachers in training to focus more time and effort studying discursive, abstract, and analytical topics *about* Christianity than witnessing in detail the lives of those who have followed Jesus in rare and creative *kingdom living*. It is also a mistake, I believe, for ministers in training to be exposed to many secondhand reports of discipleship at the expense of more hands-on practice in adventurous, selfless Christian and servant participation. We tend to be trained like all other professionals, except that our calling requires us to *be* as well as to *do!* Ministers must become living exemplars of a set of values, feelings, attitudes, loyalties, and beliefs, as well as performers. And they cannot get that altogether from a detached and derivative body of knowledge. Indeed, there *is* a body of historical and theological knowledge to be mastered, but the ministry suffers now from persons with no *arrows in their quivers,* preachers who have no sense of "Woe unto me!" nor any mandate such as ". . . thus saith the Lord!" This comes from an inward loyalty and passion for the gospel, something more than ninety semester hours and a degree. Discovery of the eternal dimension of life calls for some practice in "immortal" living and thinking and doing. The seminary must move more in the direction of being a spiritual gymnasium rather than being a center for research on effete topics *about* religion. The latter should be a program that follows for those who intend to teach.

Despite the difficulty of this challenge, we do know, and have known, people who have walked the less-traveled road and whose lives were cloaked in eternity in the midst of time. Mother Hale in Harlem has devoted a lifetime to the rearing of children with drug addiction at birth, taken as infants from Harlem Hospital and neighboring institutions. These infants have no advocates; they are unwanted, unhealthy, and unadopted. Mother Hale makes a home for them. And when she does, she steps clear of all the fears, excuses, and rationalizations that we have so easily learned to prattle; she passes from "death into life." Father Damien de Veuster of Belgium went to live with the lepers of Molokai, a small Hawaiian island, and shared their total existence, becoming a leper himself in complete identification with them and dying a leper's death. Learning about such immortal living makes eternity more real to us.

Chief Oriyinde, a Yoruba teacher educated in America, went back to Ogbomosho in Western Nigeria after graduation and spent sixty years teaching, healing, preaching, baptizing, counseling, and inspiring young lives. He did all of this without an automobile, hot running water, indoor plumbing, shopping malls, subways, drugstores, or television. *In the world* but not *of the world!*

Father Savonarola defied the corruption of the church in Florence in the fifteenth century, and he incurred the wrath of both the popes and the Medicis. In the collapse of the government, Savonarola became himself the lawgiver of Florence, and he sought to create a godly society. Opposition to him caused him constant harassment and threats to life and limb; his steadfastness brought him death by fire on the center of a cross, while his two disciples were suspended from the cross beam — one on his right and one on his left.

The knowledge of persons who have shown spiritual capacity to live an immortal life in the midst of time gives us assurance that eternity is indeed in our midst.

The preacher must somehow capture the language and the rhetoric to bring clarity and vitality to this solemn truth that we are destined to live a dual life — on the one hand living and moving chronologically in the flow of history and on the other hand existing as a spiritual being, aware of God's presence beyond time, breathing the fragrance of eternity. This dual quality of our lives is kept in balance by our constant awareness of the brevity and the transience of this mortal life and the perpetual *nowness* of immortality.

> Time, like an ever-rolling stream,
> Bears all its sons away;
> They fly forgotten, as a dream
> Dies at the opening day.[1]

If everyone else around us is immersed in contemporaneity and in the demands of the present, responding only to the crisis of the moment, the preacher is the one vested with the authority and bound by the commitment to remind us all of the eternal now that surrounds us.

---

[1]"O God, Our Help in Ages Past," by Isaac Watts.

Before the hills in order stood,
Or earth received her frame,
From everlasting Thou art God,
To endless years the same.[2]

Every Christian can testify that his or her faith in
the nearness of the kingdom of God, the brooding of
eternity over our frenetic existence, is strengthened by
the example of persons in the church who seem to have
"already passed from death into life." They are already in
Christ, dead to the old Adam, alive to the new, and they
"sit together in heavenly places in Christ Jesus." They are
in the world, working, caring for their physical necessities, being prudent about the future, charitable toward
others, enraptured with the love of God, faithful in discipleship to Jesus, and very much aware of eternity impinging upon the human condition, living in a colony of
heaven right now—*in* the world, but not *of* the world.
John said, "And this is life eternal, that they might know
thee the only true God, and Jesus Christ, whom thou has
sent" (John 17:3). They have lived changed lives right in
our presence, and they have made manifest eternal life
that shines in the midst of time.

In the city of Newark, New Jersey, a volatile economy has existed for a long time, with much of the more
well-off population leaving the older city's center for
newer, outlying developments. Many businesses have
fled, and the downward economic spiral carries everything down with it: education, civility, cleanliness, em-
ployment, and cash flow. Many of the old, large eastern
cities that were a part of America's early, rapid progress
have met the same fate. The reality is that there are
many hungry, homeless, and hopeless persons left in the
hallways, alleys, lobbies, and abandoned buildings.
Most of us see this, comment on it, feel some sense of
shame and guilt, and quickly return to our preoccupa-
tion with our carnal satisfactions.

Meanwhile, a certain Kathleen Di Chiara saw the

---

[2]Ibid.

same thing that the rest of us saw, standing in the same place and time dimension where we stand, but she allowed the transcendent influence of immortal living to guide her. She started a food bank, gathering from those who had and serving those who had not. Today her Newark food bank is the nerve center of a network of food pantries throughout New Jersey, and the hungry and homeless count on them.

The apostle Paul made this point abundantly clear when he declared:

> For those who live according to the flesh set their minds on the things of the flesh, but those who live according to the Spirit set their minds on the things of the Spirit. To set the mind on the flesh is death, but to set the mind on the Spirit is life and peace (Romans 8:5-6, RSV).

We have all been reading the same words about Jesus and the kingdom of God for a very long time, yet some church fellowships succeed in drawing their constituents into a much livelier synergism with kingdom living than do most others. It is plainly embarrassing to us who are in some of the "megadenominations" with huge budgets and staffs to meet laypersons from the Church of the Brethren, the Mennonites, the Quakers, or the Seventh Day Adventists in remote parts of the world, caring for the sick in isolated places in small dispensaries or clinics, building sewers or drainage systems, teaching in village schools, working beside farmers and fishermen, serving as midwives, or vaccinating cows and chickens.

It is humbling to hear about persons willing to surrender two years or more of their regular life's work to help persons who live in parts of the world where the environment has made life barely livable. Volunteers from the Mennonites, the Society of Friends, and other less visible fellowships feel called to defy "realism" and prudence and to answer God's call to service and discipleship. They meet extremely needy persons in their native habitation, a long way from modern technology and conveniences, and share their total experience—their

short supplies, their limitations of all sorts, and stubborn, unyielding, cultural impediments — without complaint.

It is the preacher's solemn task, as one of the em-
phases of the preaching ministry and as one of the arrows shot from his or her quiver, to assure the listeners
that our visible time and space dimensions are only one
side of our *total* existence; beyond the history that we
see and feel, there is a *parahistory,* a *metahistory,* a spiritual abode that is timeless and spaceless, an eternal
kingdom of love, peace, and genuine goodness where
God dwells, which is our spirit's true home. Getting this
across to parishioners amidst the plethora of the adver-
tisements and seductions of a sensate, hedonistic, materialistic culture is no small task.

When I studied Attic Greek in college, I learned that
the language was filled with subtleties in grammar and
vocabulary. For example, verb conjugations had the singular and the plural, just as in all languages, but there
was also the number called *dual,* only two — no more —
as another kind of plural. It is true that a plural of two is
quite different from a plural that adds any number from
one more to a million. The "dual" reflects life as it is
lived. Likewise, there was a past tense called the *aorist,*
intended to mean a "done deal," over, finished! It was
stronger than the ordinary past tense. Then, too, there
was the *optative* mood expressing a conditional act that
was more conditional, more dependent upon "other outcomes" than the subjunctive mood. It was a "should-
would" way of speaking that was deeper than a
"may-might" meaning. Life is like that, too. Not all conditional statements are equal in their reference to other
contingencies.

The other subtlety that makes us pause and ponder
is the difference between *chronos* and *kairos,* both
meaning "time." *Chronos* refers to the movement of the
sun across the horizon from east to west, gently passing
through the meridian with a steady but unhurried pace.
We measure the sun's journeyings daily with clocks and

calendars, and we accept Greenwich mean time as the correct measure. *Chronos* refers to processing the moments of time in a sequence that can be counted the same way by everybody, everywhere. *Kairos* is a different kind of time. It is not measured on the clock and calendar schedule. It refers to *a particular time* that invades our moments and our days as though eternity had dipped into history. It is like *the fullness of time,* the right time, the appointed time, God's time. God is not bound to clocks and calendars, sunrises and sunsets. God is exempt from all deadlines. God acts not according to *chronos* but at God's own time, *kairos.* So while we live in *chronos,* planting and harvesting, buying and selling, weeping and rejoicing, giving birth and dying, God is aware of all of our doings. Jesus made that clear. Not a sparrow falls to the ground without God knowing about it. But we are eligible and equipped to sense, in the midst of *chronos,* what God is doing with those *kairos* moments that dip into our days.

Some of us are better prepared than others to know the *kairos* moments when they arrive: Isaiah in the temple; Jacob at Bethel; Jeremiah with fire in his bones; Ezekiel in the valley of dry bones; Moses at Sinai; Peter, James, and John on the Mount of Transfiguration; Paul and Silas in jail in Philippi; John on Patmos; or Ruth saying to Naomi, "Intreat me not to leave thee, or to return from following after thee . . . for . . . thy people shall be my people, and thy God my God" (Ruth 1:16).

When *kairos* impinges upon *chronos,* something happens. Judgment is visited upon history, lives are changed, governments shift directions. Heaven bends low and things change. Strange events occur: the crumbling of the Berlin wall or the demise of the communist, atheist bloc in Eastern Europe or Nelson Mandela being released and South Africa beginning its rendezvous with destiny.

So when we speak of living in eternity *now,* we are speaking of relevance in a most precise respect, not of some escape from reality in a cloud of blissful oblivion.

We are talking about standing in time, like Amos, Hosea, and John the Baptist, and hearing from heaven where we are.

What are the consequences in case we should succeed at this? It just may be that more persons than we think are starving to hear a preacher who is attuned to the ways of the kingdom — *chronos* and *kairos* — standing tall, and without shame or self-righteousness, declaring the richness and beauty, the serenity and fullness of joy to be found in kingdom living. It may be that many more persons than we have imagined are bored to tears with this elusive and anxious quest for abiding satisfaction and meaning in life, chasing prizes that matter little or not at all, and they may be ready now to reach for the *real prize* of the high calling of God in Jesus Christ. The preachers themselves may be surprised to find that the *intrinsic* rewards of bringing souls to a knowledge of eternal life, here and now, may far outweigh those *extrinsic* rewards that we find so enticing.

What are the possible outcomes when the preacher lets this arrow fly? First, we expect to see many persons saved from some of the silliest, most childish idolatries in which people get lost, being helped to know that life is more than meat and raiment. When the preacher invites persons to spend an hour or so meditating on the true meaning of life, following the guidance of the Holy Spirit, in discipleship to Jesus and in the fellowship of God in the kingdom, it is a special time to become aware of the eternal dimension of our fragile and temporal existence. The preacher is under obligation to speak to this in ways that will strengthen and affirm this aspect of our being, that will help the people overcome the pressures of the week that sought to keep their noses to the grindstone, to keep them toe-to-toe with the questions of physical survival, material security, and social success. We can elbow our way through this maze seeing only numbers, hearing only the din of traffic, and getting excited about changes in the shapes of cars, the fortunes of our favorite football teams, the length of skirts, changing hairstyles, the movement of the stock market, or our weight, waistline, and the wrinkles that gather in our faces. We can be lost in a confusion of tiny idols that seize our total attention and waste our energies and affections.

It is also amazing to see how some of these idols can become obsessive. We have seen recently the candor of the press in exposing the idolatry and peccant behavior of persons of power and standing. It has become commonplace to read of a gifted and well-placed person allowing the cravings of an ego that cannot be satiated with money, fame, or power, to drag its victim into the shadows of vulgar sexual exploitation of juvenile persons who are easily curious and flattered by such attention. Often this involves adventures into perverted sex acts in which all parties revert to the denial of their basic personhood. These idols can indeed become obsessive. Others find themselves stealing more than they would ever need, as though engaged in a game, and then being brought to public disgrace.

Yet, as destructive as such idolatry is and as lamentable as the cumulation of negative consequences may be, there are still higher forms of idolatry. The most serious idolatries are those that take the glory that belongs to our eternal God and give it to temporal, ephemeral, and transitory objects that consume our highest loyalties. In our own country we offer our people the finest opportunity to create a genuine community of understanding and compassion, of pluralism and ethnic variety; but the idolatries of racism and ethnic superiority impede and frustrate such a community. We have an opportunity to employ freedom of speech, freedom of worship, freedom of the press, and government by the consent of the governed, and to present to the whole world a model peaceful, compassionate, democratic nation. But this is subverted by those who want to give "supernationalism" the place that God should have in our lives. The highest love of country should be shown by loving God first, and then by seeking to align our country's priorities to the will and purpose of God.

Otherwise the worship of nation and class is mere idolatry, like the worship of Nebuchadnezzar, Belshazzar,
Xerxes, or Caesar.

In many communities invocations are offered at
sporting events, but, curiously, not at the beginning of
the workday in the factory, at daybreak on the farm before feeding the animals, or at the wharf before unload-
ing huge ships. Why then do we invoke the presence of
the Eternal One at a game where the object is so trivial
as to get a leather ball through a metal hoop, to knock a
cloth ball over a fence, or to carry an oval ball past
eleven armored opponents and over a strip of white
paint? What makes such a trivial exercise the object of
the supervening grace of God? It is because we love a
fight, a Darwinian competition — winning, losing, raising up *ourselves* and putting down *someone else!* When
we invoke the presence of God in a football game, we as-
sume that God is a "warrior" too, and likes the same
thing.

. No one other than the preacher is charged to call us
from these silly excesses and to give the preeminence
and all the glory to a holy and a righteous God, our supreme and *wholly other* in the world, in whose presence
our souls should take delight. No one is obliged as much
as the preacher to stand clear of these idols in his or her
own life in order to be free to speak with authority, to
call our parched spirits and our thirsty souls away from
these dry wells to drink from the living waters.

Bruce A. Baldwin has pointed our attention to the
campaign that middle-class parents are engaged in to
save their children from indifferent, poor grades and
from revolt against adult leadership. This, of course, is
all about values; what we are doing is trying to bribe
children into loyalty and love. But neither love nor loyalty can be bought. The result is that we have a generation of "cornucopia kids" — kids with everything! We
have seen to it that no desire is unmet, no wish denied,
no need unanswered, no demand ignored. We are fearful
of frustrating children lest they turn to drugs, crime, or
something worse. So they are being taught a value sys-

tem that treats the world as a giant toy department, a perpetual Disneyland with no disappointments, no deferred gratifications, and no rejections. We protect them from the knowledge of and exposure to the suffering of others less fortunate than themselves. Their experiences will deny them that pensive reflection, that depth of character that adversity induces. We allow our children to grow up without a hint that there is any purpose at all in the world except their own sensate enjoyment. A community, a society, a nation, a civilization made up of persons with such rearing, "cornucopia kids," will hardly ever see the kingdom of God or experience that knowledge of God's presence that can be found only when the glitter of this world is dimmed and the noise of our clamoring is hushed.

The first practical consequence of a faithful preacher declaring the message of eternal life, the imminence of God's kingdom, and the living waters is that the people are awakened to their various idolatries and consider giving God the glory. No matter what may be happening elsewhere, no matter what other thrones there are before which other knees may be bent and other heads may be bowed, when they hear the words of eternal life they want to sing something like—

> Immortal, invisible, God only wise,
> In light inaccessible hid from our eyes,
> Most blessed, most glorious, the Ancient of Days,
> Almighty, victorious, Thy great name we praise.
>
> To all, life Thou givest, to both great and small;
> In all life Thou livest, the true life of all;
> We blossom and flourish as leaves on the tree,
> And wither and perish—but nought changeth Thee.[3]

Next, when the preacher speaks about eternity flowing through time and the nearness of God's kingdom impinging upon our lives, the people discover that

---

[3]"Immortal, Invisible, God Only Wise," by Walter Chalmers Smith.

the ways in which the society, the culture, and the historical moment have conditioned them are not the ultimate influences. They discover that it is possible to make contact with this higher dimension of life, the eternal presence and power of the living God, and transcend the conditioning that temporal institutions have imposed upon us.

When Paul was on his second missionary journey, he came to Philippi, a city Luke described as a colony in Macedonia, an imperial Roman city where the government was delegated directly from Rome. Like all colonies, the uniforms, coins, salutes, insignia, architecture, and conversation all reflected the mores, laws, customs, and practices of the motherland, headquarters. Philippi looked different from other towns; it had less local flavor and more of the flavor of Rome itself. But when Paul wrote to the Christians there, he said to them, "Our commonwealth is in heaven . . ." (Philippians 3:20). This can be paraphrased, "Our citizenship is in heaven." While we, like the Philippians, may claim that we are citizens of a certain city, state, or country, we are also a colony of heaven, bound by the ways of God's kingdom, greeting one another, not in the name of Caesar, but in the name of Christ, and behaving not so much to please Caesar as to please God.

When the mainline clergy of Birmingham asked Martin Luther King, Jr., to change the tempo of his struggle for justice from *allegro* to *largo*, to slow down, they were not speaking as though God had spoken to them. They had muted the words of eternal life and were echoing the voices of a society that had grown comfortable subjugating, embarrassing, ignoring, and denying persons on the basis of their color. They were pleading for an inhumane, unjust system to last a little longer, for the pain and hurt to continue until those who had grown calloused to it were at last—whenever!—ready to allow it to subside. This is all the more confusing because these preachers talked and sang and prayed about the cross all the time, and the only cross they seemed to recognize was the *gold* one dangling from a *gold* chain!

The fact is that if we tuned our messages more to the vibrations of God's eternal kingdom, we would hear not only what King heard about the urgency of altering racial injustice, but also what God is calling us to be— more prophetic about the desperate poor in our country and in the world, about the chronic failure of our educational system to induct neglected youth into the life of the mind, and about the awful disparity in the economic rewards and favors that we permit in this nation "under God." One man earned over $17 million in one year as an automobile executive while our cars were characterized as the most poorly built in the world! The silence on such issues in our exquisite air-conditioned, cushioned, and carpeted sanctuaries punctuates the distance between us and the herald of the kingdom who preached in the wilderness of Judea, wearing a loincloth, eating locusts and honey, crying that the kingdom was at hand, that *kairos* was visiting *chronos*.

When the preacher proclaims the ever-present potential of God's kingdom and the flow of eternity through our existence, the people get the message that the way this temporal dimension has shaped our lives is not the final word. We are indeed a colony of heaven, and we have other connections.

The practice of segregating black worshipers began in the colonial churches in America. They were made to sit in balcony seats or behind a screen or a wall, and they received the Communion wine from separate chalices. Society had already reduced blacks to slave status, and all of the other relationships with blacks had to correspond with this subhuman designation. Some blacks accepted their status, but others rejected such a definition of themselves. They had read about Daniel defying the king and serving his God, about Ezekiel preaching to dry bones in Babylon, about Nehemiah rebuilding the city for the return of the exiles, and about John of Patmos having a vision of the New Jerusalem. So while their *bodies* were enslaved, their *spirits* dwelt in lofty places.

Therefore, when the Christians who controlled the

churches tried to impose the status of slaves on the
blacks who came to worship in Philadelphia, South
Carolina, Georgia, Virginia, and New York, the black
Christians heard from heaven, where their real citizenship was, and they walked out of those churches, assert-
ing their dignity as members of the colony of heaven. In
Philadelphia they founded the African Methodist Episcopal Church; in New York in the Wall Street neighbor-
hood they founded the Abyssinian Baptist Church.
Others were established in Norfolk, Charleston, Richmond, Savannah, and Petersburg at nearly the same
time and in the same way.

The black church has often been criticized for being
too "heavenward," too other-worldly; and the black
preacher has been criticized for failing to emphasize the
present physical well-being of the people. This is a curious complaint, given the fact that black preachers and
black church-funded schools created the educated
black leadership class from 1865 on into this century.
The black preachers have been the vanguard of the civil
rights movement. There are three black preachers in
Congress and another who almost won the Democratic
nomination for president. There is a balance, however,
that has to be guarded: black persons are just as subject
to all the conditions of kingdom living as any others and
are just as eligible to live with an immortal dimension to
their lives as anyone else. And this kingdom dwelling
calls all of us, in the Spirit of Christ, away from empty
piety to a vital involvement in the needs and the concerns of the "least of these." Living in the kingdom is not
removal from service and response to human need; it is
a tighter, closer, deeper involvement, following the leadership of Jesus.

A new definition of our personhood is also found in
eternal life. In Christ we are new creations. Jesus told
Nicodemus that we could be born anew in the Spirit.
How many of us have found the most meaningful personal counseling in a sermon that boldly declared this
newness of life found in God's kingdom, a freedom that
was conferred by the eternal Spirit of God?

How shall they hear? They will listen for a word
that will release them from the fetters that have bound
them, that will offer them an option more viable than
cocaine and alcohol, that will enable them to rise above
their temporal antecedents and conditioning, their negative and distorted definitions of themselves, and set
them free. Fanny Crosby was blind in this temporal,
physical dimension of life, but as a citizen in the colony
of heaven she sang,

> Thou, my everlasting portion,
> More than friend or life to me;
> All along my pilgrim journey,
> Saviour, let me walk with Thee.[4]

If eternity is real and if God is alive, our ways of
knowing about such things, our epistemology, should
leave room for the flooding of the mind with new truth,
not only objective, cold facts about biology, physics, astronomy, or organic chemistry, but the truth about
God's love in special circumstances, God's direction in
crisis situations, God's hand reaching into history to create novelty—completely new "for instances" and unprec-
edented change. In order for preachers to demonstrate
how we can be free of the fetters of our "nowness," our
obligations to the culture and historical-causal determination, we must learn to walk in that spiritual transcen-
dence that Jesus taught us first. We must feel eternity
bending low all around us.

However, perhaps most importantly it is the presence of God that enables us in a very practical way to
endure when our strength is inadequate and the burdens are really too heavy for us to bear. Something happens, for example, in those small rural churches in
dusty hollows and in storefronts in urban America every
Sunday morning and many nights during the week that
should happen in every church. Burdens are lightened,
and the easy yoke of Christ is found. In places where

---

[4]"Close to Thee," by Fanny J. Crosby.

there is no sign of sophistication, someone learned,
somehow, what the prophet meant when he said:

> Hast thou not known? hast thou not heard, that the everlasting
> God, the LORD, the Creator of the ends of the earth, fainteth not,
> neither is weary? there is no searching of his understanding. He
> giveth power to the faint; and to them that have no might he in-
> creaseth strength. Even the youths shall faint and be weary, and
> the young men shall utterly fall; But they that wait upon the LORD
> shall renew their strength; they shall mount up with wings as ea-
> gles; they shall run, and not be weary; and they shall walk, and not
> faint (Isaiah 40:28–31).

It is true, also, that often persons can too soon be
led to resign lazily from challenges and opportunities to
grow, to take their burdens to the Lord and leave them
there without any hard effort at all on their own part.
The preacher must be careful not to encourage sloth, in-
dolence, or escapism. But here we are acknowledging
that when all human resources are spent, when every
live option has been canvassed, life can lead us into dismal swamps and swelling tides. We need deliverance;
we need a parting of the waters from on high. When the
preacher assures us that the breath of the Lord will
breathe on us and that there is a balm in Gilead, this
may be the most needful message to be heard.

Only a pastor who lives close to the needs of the
people can know what heroism there is in the lives of so
many uncelebrated persons and how many persons have
found adequacy to cope with life's rough places only in
the life of prayer, communing with God, and getting a
taste of eternity every Sunday morning. Many persons
have no idea what a counselor is and have never seen
one. They have no image of a psychiatrist at work. What
they do know is how tangled the threads of their lives
can become, what empty feelings overcome them from
time to time, and how exhausted they are as they drag
themselves from one long sleepless night to the other.
And they know that they have been able to shut out the
present world and do what the slaves called "steal away
to Jesus."

Something comparable to that experience we must make available to persons reared in cold and stolid empiricism, who speak the language of modernity, who live with the miracles of science and technology every day, but whose inner lives have lost all meaning and wholeness, all joy and solace, and who need an experience of eternity invading time and the feeling of sweet surrender to God in Jesus Christ.

So, when the preacher reaches into his or her quiver and lets this arrow fly—when a message is brought to the people on the reality of eternity in the midst of time, on the imminence of God's kingdom—at least three results are accomplished: The people are called from their wasteful idolatry; they are given the freedom to transcend the negative antecedents in their lives; and they are brought into the orbit of God's power and enabled to cope with the strains and tensions of life. Nothing is more important than to find release from empty idols and senseless loyalties, to find freedom from our worst influences, and to find peace for a troubled mind.

There remains one last challenge with which we all must reckon; this becomes the preacher's most singular opportunity. No one else is expected to be so well prepared to stand by with a word of truth and significance when the curtains of life are drawn on our final act. No mission in our ministry calls for greater seriousness than to stand by in the hour of deepest sorrow and to know the right word to say—or not to say—to help a broken heart find healing and comfort. The very presence of the pastor ought to recapitulate in the mind of the one who mourns those deep truths about eternal life that bring profound meaning to this moment.

It is absolutely vulgar the way some funerals are ripped through, like ordering lunch or changing a tire. Words of eulogy and committal should never be uttered with such detachment that they forfeit the most helpful ministry available to persons at their most helpless moment.

Death is a time of unique specificity and detail. Let me be personal. On January 15, 1978, I awakened in the

early morning hours in a drenching sweat with a
wrenching chest pain and a parched throat. My fading
consciousness told me that it was a heart attack; it was a
myocardial infarction. In one existential moment I
rolled through the reels of the passing of my days from
Huntersville and Mr. Petty's ice wagon to the lively adventure of raising four sons. I connected in seconds with
the entire collection of gracious souls in Norfolk, Petersburg, and Richmond, Virginia; Providence, Rhode Island; Greensboro, North Carolina; Lagos, Nigeria;
Wisconsin, New Jersey, and New York City who had
cheered me on my way. Time seemed to stand still as my
memory recapitulated fifty-seven years of traveling this
lonesome valley. My wife scurried to get an ambulance,
and I noted that her partnership was as it had been for
thirty-four years—a known quantity, fixed and unquestioned. I was sure that the final curtain was slowly being
drawn, and a release came over me. Strangely I had no
fear, no fretfulness, no hesitation, no reluctance in giving up this world. I earnestly believed that those whis-
pers of eternity that had accompanied my days were
evidences of something better to come. I would lay down
this robe of flesh and clay and be free.

    It was not to be then, however, and twelve years
later while vacationing with family and friends, I lost
my breath. Another coronary artery had closed, and
open-heart surgery was required. My routine of preparation for departure was in place again, and the same
quiet, firm resignation accompanied me. There is nothing like the isolation of that moment of judgment when
one feels that a lifetime of choosing and selecting, trying
and failing, sinning and repenting, winning and losing,
weeping and rejoicing, must be summarized and reported on, when there is no time for further corrections.
There is no feeling like tying up the loose ends of long
and happy associations and ending abruptly those relationships that we lean on every day. It was almost over.
And there is no feeling like knowing that the Christ of
faith is just as alive as the Jesus of history was in Judea
and Galilee, and that he has prepared a place for us.

There is no feeling like knowing that our sins and short-comings are no embarrassment to God because the grace that was shed abroad from Calvary was God's own initiative to assure us the final victory.

Well, it would be unbearable and heart-rending, and we could not endure the pain of erasing so much in one stroke if our faith in the presence of God in this world and the next were feeble. The preacher must know that sermons that affirm immortal life provide the underpinning that holds all of this together. This one life, the only life that we are allowed, has run its course, and what we believe lies ahead makes all the difference in the world. If we have no spiritual continuity and all of this is reduced to dust and ashes and a fading dream, it seems like the worst trick that could be played on anyone. But if we have been taught to listen for the songs of angels and to hear heavenly voices ringing, "we wrap the draperies of our couch about us and lie down to pleasant dreams." We hear the Master saying, "I am the resurrection and the life...whosoever liveth and believeth in me shall never die" (John 11:25a, 26a).

We have done our best when we have established in the hearts of our people that the psalmist said it all:

I had fainted, unless I had believed to see the goodness of the LORD in the land of the living (Psalm 27:13).

Some careers are devoted to the health of the human body, some to the practical needs of our transportation from one locus to another, and some to creating aesthetic enjoyment as we witness the talent and genius of the gifted ones. Other careers make provision for our need for food, education, housing, and environmental protection—safety from storm and flood. Some careers monitor our broader mutual interests and protect us from excesses and violations against one another—lawyers, legislators, arbitrators of all sorts, geopoliticians, and macroeconomists. The preacher of the gospel of the Son of God acknowledges all of these needs and services and seeks to lead the people beyond them toward coherence, to profound and deep meaning in their lives, and to abiding commitments. Through the gift, the art, and the craft of the preacher, in pursuit of the highest calling of all, we are made aware of a God who intervenes in our behalf; we recognize our potential for renewal and reconciliation with God; we affirm the possibility of a genuine community; and we strengthen our trust in whom we have believed. We can say: "I know whom I have believed, and am persuaded that he is able to keep that which I have committed unto him" (2 Timothy 1:12).